More Praise for *Completing C*

"Courageously reconciles dimensions that were thought to be mutually exclusive for centuries. A must-read for today's business leaders who are ready to reinvent their world!"

—Jean-Christophe Flatin, President, Mars Global Chocolate

"Roche and Jakub dramatically succeed where others have dismally failed. Their clear, concise, values-driven words shape capitalism into its final form and elevate it to the pinnacle position that it deserves. Roche's and Jakub's superb scholarship is underpinned and supported by the practical reality of successful pilots and business world applications. They not only complete capitalism, they create and hand us a road map for responsible business in the 21st century."

—Dr. Frank Akers, former Associate Director, Oak Ridge National Laboratory; Chairman, Mars Science Advisory Council; CEO, Oak Ridge Strategies Group; and Brigadier General, US Army (ret.)

"For Veolia, the world leader in environmental services, the question of innovation in service of human progress is central: expanding access to natural resources, preserving and renewing them is our vocation. Our values at Veolia are in profound harmony with the great essay of *Completing Capitalism*, which proposes a vision and practical solutions for a responsible capitalism based on reciprocity and shared prosperity."

—Dinah Louda, Executive Director, Veolia Institute, and advisor to the CEO of Veolia

"The more complete form of capitalism put forward by Roche and Jakub is not about competitive advantage. But to be competitive in the future, companies will need to operate this way."

—Paul Michaels, former CEO, Mars, Incorporated, and former executive, Johnson & Johnson and Procter & Gamble

"Some endeavors require intellectual, emotional, or spiritual courage. Bruno and Jay have demonstrated all three in fleshing out this valuable piece of work on behalf of Mars, Incorporated, our associates, and all stakeholders, including the planet. I truly hope it evolves, as I believe it can and must, the dialogue regarding capitalism's future and its crucial role in our world going forward."

—Stephen Badger, Chairman of the Board, Mars, Incorporated

"As human beings we long for the way the world is supposed to be, even as we make choices against that hope. For years Roche and Jakub have been hard at work rethinking the way that business should be and ought to be—if we are to flourish as selves and societies, choosing a future that understands the grain of the universe. With a rare willingness to ask the most critical questions about the nature of business, their 'economics of mutuality' is a vision for doing good and doing well in the context of one of the most iconic brands in the modern world. Neither charity nor corporate social responsibility, but rather a way for sustained profitability, this book argues for making money in a way that remembers the meaning of the marketplace."

—Dr. Steven Garber, Principal, The Washington Institute, and author of *Visions of Vocation* and *The Fabric of Faithfulness*

"This crisis is more than a 'normal' crisis. It requires a reset of our thoughts and ways of doing. Business as usual does not work anymore or anywhere. The journey that Jakub and Roche are proposing is a difficult one but a promising and fecund one. It is ambitious but within our reach to make this world a better one. This is, I believe, the only reasonable option. We have patched up the system. This is the good news. We have to rebuild. This is the promising appeal. A properly functioning market economy must work for the many, not just for the few. Now is the time if we want to eradicate poverty in our generation. And here is how."

—Bertrand Badré, CEO, BlueOrange Capital; former Managing Director and Chief Financial Officer, World Bank Group; and former Group Chief Financial Officer, Société Générale and Crédit Agricole

"Institutions today are failing to adjust to the urgent needs of humanity. Power has shifted to MNCs. Therefore, the responsibility for sustainable human existence lies mainly on the shoulders of business leaders. Roche and Jakub address the right questions, economic and spiritual, while providing a vision and practical approach for making profits together with serving social, natural, and human needs. Their book invites us to engage in a paradigm shift. It calls for a movement of moral, responsible business leaders. Let's move forward!"

—Avishay Braverman, former Senior Economist and Division Chief, World Bank; former President, Ben-Gurion University; and former Cabinet Minister and Chair, Finance and Economic Affairs Committees, Knesset

Completing Capitalism
Heal Business to Heal the World

Bruno Roche ❖ Jay Jakub

Berrett–Koehler Publishers, Inc.
a BK Business book

Berrett-Koehler Publishers, Inc.
1333 Broadway, Suite 1000
Oakland, CA 94612-1921
Tel: (510) 817-2277   Fax: (510) 817-2278   www.bkconnection.com

Ordering Information

Quantity sales. Special discounts are available on quantity purchases by corporations, associations, and others. For details, contact the "Special Sales Department" at the Berrett-Koehler address above.

Individual sales. Berrett-Koehler publications are available through most bookstores. They can also be ordered directly from Berrett-Koehler: Tel: (800) 929-2929; Fax: (802) 864-7626; www.bkconnection.com

Orders for college textbook/course adoption use. Please contact Berrett-Koehler: Tel: (800) 929-2929; Fax: (802) 864-7626.

Orders by U.S. trade bookstores and wholesalers. Please contact Ingram Publisher Services, Tel: (800) 509-4887; Fax: (800) 838-1149; E-mail: customer.service@ ingrampublisherservices.com; or visit www.ingrampublisherservices.com/Ordering for details about electronic ordering.

Berrett-Koehler and the BK logo are registered trademarks of Berrett-Koehler Publishers, Inc.

Printed in the United States of America

Berrett-Koehler books are printed on long-lasting acid-free paper. When it is available, we choose paper that has been manufactured by environmentally responsible processes. These may include using trees grown in sustainable forests, incorporating recycled paper, minimizing chlorine in bleaching, or recycling the energy produced at the paper mill.

Library of Congress Cataloging-in-Publication Data
Names: Roche, Bruno, (Economist) author. | Jakub, Jay, author.
Title: Completing capitalism : heal business to heal the world / Bruno Roche, Jay Jakub.
Description: First Edition. | Oakland : Barrett-Koehler Publishers, [2017]
Identifiers: LCCN 2016059032 | ISBN 9781626569270 (pbk.)
Subjects: LCSH: Capitalism. | Capital market. | Human capital. | Infrastructure (Economics)
Classification: LCC HB501 .R6293 2017 | DDC 330.12/2--dc23
LC record available at https://lccn.loc.gov/2016059032

22 21 20 19 18 17   10 9 8 7 6 5 4 3 2 1

Interior design and production: Dovetail Publishing Services
Cover designer: Cassandra Chu

To the author and perfecter of our faith

Contents

Foreword

Colin Mayer, *Oxford University*

Martin Radvan, *Mars, Incorporated*

Oxford University entered into Mars' mutuality journey three years ago when Bruno Roche and Jay Jakub together with a team from Mars Catalyst came to the Saïd Business School to give a presentation on what they called the "economics of mutuality."[1] Of course, we had some notion of the innovative management practices in which Mars was engaged but we had no idea of what we were about to hear. The effect was electrifying. People in the business school came away thinking that there was really something of substance that warranted careful and in-depth analysis. So the seeds for what has thus far been a two-year—and is destined to be a many year—collaborative research program between Oxford University and Mars, Incorporated were sown.

We started in earnest in October 2014 examining what this curious concept of mutuality meant in practice within Mars. We talked to people at all levels in the organization and in particular focused on a pilot study in Nairobi, Kenya, called Maua, in which Mars Catalyst (Mars' internal corporate think tank) was actively engaged. What I came to realize were three things.

First, that mutuality was a process, not a realization. It was the exploration of the way in which business can implement structures, systems, and practices to derive benefits through conferring benefits. Mars was in the process of identifying these structures, systems, and practices through experimentation, observation, and learning.

Second, and as a consequence, academia and business had a considerable amount to contribute to as well as learn from each other. In essence, quite correctly, Mars appreciated that business was not about knowing but learning, and since academia is about researching and informing, there is a natural partnership between the two. Companies appreciate that they have a great deal to gain from the scientific and technical knowledge of universities, but few understand that there is a benefit from partnering with them in the discovery of new business practices as well.

Third, the nature of that partnership between academia and business is itself mutual in nature. The interests of business and academia are not naturally aligned. Business is immediate, private, and confidential; academia is long term, public, and open. The reason the two coexist as distinct entities is because of their differences. Forging a relationship therefore requires an unusual appreciation of the goals, constraints, and attributes of the two parties and an avoidance of a condemnation of their respective failings.

In that regard, the Saïd Business School at Oxford University was extremely fortunate to have been able to partner with Mars Catalyst, the think tank of Mars, which, as an organization that combines the research and practice of management, was able to offer the intermediation between the academic and business world that was required for the project to flourish. In particular, as the leaders of Mars Catalyst, Bruno Roche and Jay Jakub provided the vision, imagination, and leadership that were required to bring the program to fruition.

Like mutuality, the research program is a journey on which we have learned not only about mutuality in business but also about how to promote mutuality in business research. What this book represents is a remarkable description of the concepts that underlie that program and the journey by which those ideas have emerged. It is a story that is of immense importance in understanding what is required to reform business in the twenty-first century because, as we are all coming to appreciate, the failings of business are impoverishing us not just economically and financially but as individuals and societies.

Reforming business is essential not only for completing capitalism but preserving it as well. We have seen only too clearly over the last few years the political as well as social ramifications of our failure to do that. We have made remarkably little progress, and time is running out before distrust and mistrust rise to a point where the fabric of our economies that we take for granted will be eroded.

This book provides us with the basis for understanding what needs to be done and what business can do. We should all take heed and learn the essential lessons that it seeks to teach us.

Colin Mayer, *former dean, Oxford University's Saïd Business School (SBS); Peter Moores Professor of Management Studies, SBS; author of* Firm Commitment: How the Corporation Is Failing Us and How to Restore Trust In It

My journey discovering the economics of mutuality had humble origins starting with my own employment as a very junior associate in the Mars company more than thirty years ago. Initially my understanding was limited to a very simple relationship between myself and the company—I worked hard and I received new career opportunities and progressed financially. During the business period of rapid geographic expansion, I then witnessed firsthand what an enormous difference a successful business can make to all of its stakeholders, including employees, suppliers, customers, and a myriad of their dependents and networks.

Experiencing this very tangible, indeed visual, impact of shared benefits in a variety of geographies from the Middle East to Central Europe left me in no doubt of the underlying and fundamental truth in the principle.

During my time managing the Catalyst function, I was exposed to the "what is the right level of profit" question and resulting research. This in turn seeded thoughts and a deep personal curiosity as to whether one could measure or even perhaps quantify our impact beyond financial measures and then indeed influence the delivery of that impact.

On assuming leadership of the beverages division of Mars, it was of course clear that rapid growth of this business was an imperative. But in addition to growth with all its inherent benefits, another question loomed: Could we drive a course of action to benefit specific stakeholders, and would such action enable us to realize the "biggest bang for our buck"? With the help of the authors' analysis of shared value, a crystal clear "call to arms" emerged. The coffee growers at the very start of our value chain deserved the most attention. Personal visits to these source geographies only reinforced this conviction. As relatively small buyers of the total coffee crop, we had the luxury to decide where to buy from and hence where to focus our attention. In combination with our financial capital measures, human, social, and natural capital measures allowed us to select where we had the best prospects for success and enabled empirical measurement of our progress. The prospect of setting a business target of X% growth, in addition to Y% improvement in "social capital" of the growers, came in sight. In addition to the personal motivation this delivered, I was overwhelmed by the general engagement this generated within my management team and many other involved associates.

When I moved to run the William Wrigley Co. (a division of Mars), I carried these formative ideas with me. Within the Wrigley value chain we identified mint farming as a potential opportunity. However the same value chain analysis revealed that in the case of gum, a much larger opportunity lay in improving the share of prosperity within our distribution network—specifically in emerging markets. With Kenya as a fertile ground for experimentation, we set about testing our ability to generate micro-entrepreneurs. Our first attempts were abortive and taught us many hard lessons, but slowly, with the help of local partners, we established improved methodologies and rapidly we were able to foster some very promising results. Strict attention to deployment methodology and rigorous scientific discipline in measuring the impact allowed us to refine our approach, improve our operations, and start to measure our impact on the society in the areas of downtown Nairobi in which we worked. No experience can be more personally humbling yet motivating than meeting our entrepreneurs—for example a young mother who had moved her income from subsistence to a level where she could support her children's education.

We have subsequently rolled this out into other areas (e.g., the Philippines), and we now have very exciting test programs in rural China, including the use of new e-technology to measure our impact.

Sadly we cannot right all the wrongs and injustice in our world, but through the approach outlined by the authors I am convinced that we can and we do make a significant difference to many, many lives along our value chain. Therefore my fervent wish is that we simply continue to share, learn, and accelerate our progress.

Martin Radvan, *President, Mars Wrigley Confectionery*

Introduction

Uprooting the Dysfunctions of Financial Capitalism

In a real sense all life is interrelated. All men are caught in an inescapable network of mutuality, tied in a single garment of destiny. Whatever affects one directly, affects all indirectly. I can never be what I ought to be until you are what you ought to be, and you can never be what you ought to be until I am what I ought to be ... This is the interrelated structure of reality.

Martin Luther King, Jr.

It all started with an unusual question ...

More than a year before the 2008 financial crisis, the global food and beverage company Mars, Incorporated, asked what the right level of profit should be for its business activities.

Although this question has been pondered by mankind for several thousands of years ...

A man may give freely, and still his wealth will be increased; and another may keep back more than is right, but only comes to be in need. (King Solomon, 950 BC)

... it has been acted upon in a very particular way since the early 1970s by the adherents of renowned economist Milton Friedman and his Chicago School of Economics. The Friedman model called "financial capitalism" has become dominant

1

across the business world, and can be very briefly summarized as follows:

> *There is one and only one social responsibility of business— to use its resources and engage in activities designed to increase its profits [for shareholders].*

In that context, the question about the "right level of profit" is remarkable in the sense that it was posed by a corporation rather than a stakeholder or by an altruistic outside observer. It also occurred one year before the 2008 global financial crisis, and it directly challenged the core hypothesis of the dominant school of thought of Chicago.

The 2008 crisis began a questioning of the relevancy of the Chicago school

Since the 2008 crisis, the question of balancing people, planet, and profit has become a growing field of interest for an increasing number of stakeholders (businesses, NGOs, academics, etc.), denoting a rising level of discomfort with the current model. The majority of related initiatives in this space have focused on either mainstream corporate social responsibility (CSR) initiatives to attenuate or mitigate the negative impact of business on society and the environment, or on setting up philanthropic foundations or social impact–type funds to focus on social and environmental issues on the periphery of the business, or on social and environmental issues unrelated to business. But neither of these has truly challenged the system at its core or has challenged whether the "right" level of profit may not be the level that maximizes shareholder value unconditionally.

The right level of profit and two corollary questions

The question of the right level of profit raised two other important questions for us in our work that are both pragmatic and ethical. The first is whether there is an optimum level of profit that can ensure maximization of the holistic value created by the firm, including the continuing, healthy, profitable development of the firm. The second asks what moral principles might justify how much value a firm can extract from the business ecosystem in which it operates and upon which its long-term development depends. Both questions begin to address how value creation, value concentration, and value sharing are or should be related to one another.

These two questions—about holistic value optimization and morals, respectively—ultimately opened the door for an extensive applied research program (called the economics of mutuality[1]) that encouraged us to think big about how business (especially multinational corporations, or MNCs) could become a restorative power to address societal and environmental issues.

The program we embarked upon[2] has combined academic research with thought-leading academic institutions and a strong business focus with Mars as a main sponsor, and it is now growing with the involvement of other MNCs that see value in our approach.

Visions of the authors

Completing Capitalism presents some of the most insightful ideas and results coming from our ongoing applied research program to date. The program, in our view and in the opinion of an increasing number of businesspeople, academics, and other thought leaders with whom we are now collaborating, may constitute a major business breakthrough. But this book is meant to introduce the new approach we propose rather than to detail it in depth. Such a book will actually come next year, coauthored with our key academic partners. This is, in part, because we are still very much on a journey of discovery ourselves, meaning the program continues to move ahead with new business pilots, partnerships, and findings every day. Still, there is much detail to share right now, and we have done so in these pages to illustrate the new model sufficiently for the reader to grasp its basic components and understand how it functions in practice.

This book also does not reflect the official position of Mars, Incorporated, but rather represents the informed perspective of the authors, who have jointly led this research effort since 2007 in their management leadership roles within the Mars internal think tank called Catalyst. We worked on the program collaboratively with our corporate think tank colleagues, and with a wide range of business leaders, NGOs, and external experts from a number of universities around the world and across many academic disciplines. We are telling the story, but there were many other protagonists and supporting cast involved without whom we would not be writing this today.

The crux of our discovery—in brief

Our approach is based on the simple assumption that most business sustainability issues can be solved effectively and durably, not through ad hoc CSR initiatives or philanthropy, but through innovative business model approaches that have the ability to drive both social and environmental performance while also delivering strong financial performance. The management theory we are developing, therefore, holds that business can simultaneously drive both profits and wider mutual benefits to people and planet through understanding and managing multiple forms of capital, namely human, social, natural, and shared financial capital. It is based on the assumption that while good management of these capitals can drive superior business performance, business in return can also impact (positively or negatively) these capitals.

The methodological challenge we have had to address essentially is twofold. First, the new metrics for the new forms of capital must be simple enough to be enacted in a business context, and stable across different geographies and business situations. Second, these metrics must be actionable for companies through new business practices and must deliver both social and environmental performance, along with excellent financial performance. Absent the aforementioned, we would frankly add little to traditional CSR approaches to business sustainability that deliver some good for society and/or the environment (or some "less bad"), at a cost to shareholder dividend, meaning the application would not likely hold the potential for business reformation.

While extensive research and major breakthrough insights have been accomplished on the measurement side (see table I.1), the development of new business practices to enact these new forms of capital that will lead to truly holistic business performance is still largely a green field that we are currently developing and testing. Table I.1 is a summary of the major insights we have uncovered through our program thus far that can begin to provide business with core drivers of performance that go beyond financial capital.

Table I-1. Key Findings: Other Forms of Capital and How They can be Measured

Human Capital	
Key drivers of individual well-being in any cultural context based on individual skills, experience, knowledge, satisfaction (general and job specific), and health.	Measured through an adapted "well-being at work" survey to guide human resource–type interventions that will bring tangible benefits in talent attraction, retention, and optimization of performance.
Social Capital	
Nonfinancial relationships that affect a community's well-being and prosperity in ways that can bring sustainable quality of life increases which, in turn, positively impact performance.	Measured by survey through just three key drivers in any business situation or location: trust, community cohesion, and capacity for collective action.
Natural Capital	
The complete input flow of natural resources used across the entire value chain of a product.	Measured through five main metrics: materials (renewable and nonrenewable), air, water, and topsoil erosion, the granular understanding of which can guide management investment decisions to make businesses more resource efficient.
Shared Financial Capital	
How economic benefits of business activities are shared among a value chain's participants, in order to ensure a sustainable margin and wage and to identify where supply chains are comparatively strong or vulnerable.	Measured in economic value created locally and in the wider community.

These metrics have four crucial characteristics in common that are designed to ensure business relevance and broad applicability:

❖ **Parsimonious.** Each capital can be measured with a small number of variables accounting for approximately 75 percent of each of the capitals (good enough and simple enough for business use).

❖ **Related to performance.** The strong correlation between nonfinancial capitals with economic performance has been established in a number of our business pilots across geographies and business situations.

❖ **Stable.** They are stable across several countries (in Africa, Asia), different businesses, and different situations and value chains (supply and demand side).

❖ **Actionable.** The data collected offers managers "levers" that can be pulled to address pain points in the business ecosystem. Further, longitudinal data shows that the capitals can be affected—positively and/or negatively—by business interventions.

A more detailed description of these metrics and how they work in business situations to bring enhanced holistic performance is detailed in subsequent chapters of this book.

Why we focus on multinational corporations

We chose to test our new model initially in an MNC context because MNCs have become over time the strongest force in society, surpassing in many ways the power of nation-states, which are more limited in their power and reach than ever before. This is because of huge debt burdens on governments and limited geographic access typically confined to physical borders (unlike the MNC, which can operate almost everywhere). In addition, MNCs (along with some very large foundations) are today the most important actors in our increasingly globalized world, in the sense that only they have sufficient capacity to truly embrace global issues in potentially transformational ways and to address head-on the most acute pain points in our society, such as good job creation, rebuilding communities, and replenishing natural resources, among others. No other organizations have this capacity.

Our strategic priority from the beginning of this project has been twofold: (1) to offer business tools and methods to drive enhanced holistic performance that is more mutually beneficial to all stakeholders and, therefore, could be more sustainable long term than the present model of profit maximization for shareholders alone; and (2) to influence how businesses at large manage their performance (heal business) to positively impact society and the environment (heal the world). Changing MNC business models to make them more universally sustainable—by being better aligned with the new values and "rules of the game" of the emerging knowledge economy, where leveraging relationships for access to information is of more value than just accumulating financial capital (money)—can be the way by which capitalism itself can be reformed (or, as we suggest in the title of this book, completed). As we will explain, this will take place through a new approach to value creation, codified in a business model that is underpinned by robust science and rooted in a new management theory.

The journey

As we began to kick off the journey, we questioned whether an unremitting focus on driving profit up in the short term— often at the expense of other parties involved in the production of wealth—is truly profitable in the longer term. We wanted to explore whether rebalancing business priorities to give greater consideration to individuals, communities, and natural resources might actually deliver greater rewards in the future— perhaps even becoming the basis for a new business model for the new century we have entered.

Three inputs needed to nurture economic development . . . but not remunerated equally

We started by looking back in history, noting that there have always been three basic inputs that were needed to nurture economic development and that required remuneration: the planet that provides natural resources, the people who transform those resources to create something of value, and the money or profit (financial capital) whose purpose is primarily to ensure liquidity in the system. Historically, money was never meant to be used as an instrument to enable the infinite accumulation of wealth. But each of these inputs—planet, people, profit—have been remunerated in very different ways depending on the historical era and on the prevailing economic school of thought in that era.

Marxism, for example, proposed to remunerate people, which eventually took place in uneven ways at the expense of profit and of the health of the planet. Financial capitalism of the Friedman ilk, by contrast, rewards the holders of financial capital at the expense of people (the many)—unless they are shareholders (the few)—and at the expense of the planet. And some today propose to remunerate the planet at the expense of financial capital and of people. Our view is that in order to build a truly sustainable business, we need to develop a model that accounts for the value that each input brings to the business, and for how the business accounts for (measures, manages, values) each of these inputs, including how business grows or diminishes them,

9

how these inputs are related to one another (links that exist, if any), and how they contribute to the holistic value created by the firm.

The new (questionable) value of money in recent times

It is interesting to note that the last of the three inputs we observe—money—has actually been remarkably stable in its function up until recently. From the time of ancient Egypt until the late eighteenth century, for example, money was mostly a unit of payment and an instrument of liquidity, not the preferred instrument to store value. The land, later followed by the industrial means of production, was the primary instrument to store value.

The etymologic meaning of the word "capital" actually confirms this. It comes from the Latin word capus, meaning the head, referring to heads of cattle (note that it gave us the French word cheptel, meaning literally livestock). Capital in its rudimentary form was therefore understood to be an instrument to bring liquidity into the system to transport wealth from one geographical location to another and/or from one point in time to another. It was not meant to be a unit of accumulation (store of value).

It is only recently that the definition of money changed, moving from being a unit of payment and instrument of liquidity to become altogether an instrument to store value (almost infinitely). It has also become an instrument of speculation, accounting for more than 98 percent of all foreign exchange, with the risk that this change of identity may have eroded almost entirely its intrinsic value. Even more recently, as a response to the global financial crisis of 2008, central banks of developed economies have launched a series of unconventional monetary policies called quantitative easing (QE), whereby a central bank creates new money electronically to buy financial assets, such as government bonds, with the aim of directly supporting the economy by increasing private sector spending and fighting deflation (or simply returning the level of inflation to a desired target).

The amount of financial capital liquidity that has been added to the world financial system through multiple rounds of QE stimulus by central banks in developed countries has increased dramatically since 2008 and is staggering by any form of measure. In aggregate, for example, the balance sheets of the central banks of the United States, Europe, Japan, and England have expanded by almost $4 trillion from 2011 to 2014—almost $1 trillion per year since the end of 2010. And the global money supply is continuing to grow. In mid-2016, a new record was reached at $180 billion injected into the economic system every month, and in October 2016, the International Monetary Fund reported that global debt reached a record $152 trillion—more than twice the value of the entire global economy. Many market analysts now predict that the QE trend will continue, with the European Central Bank, the Bank of Japan, and even the Bank of England (to compensate for the costs of the so-called "Brexit" vote—Britain's now impending exit from the European Union) all expected to expand their QE programs with the aim of supporting fragile growth and pushing low inflation to somewhat higher levels.

The creation of so much new money from nothing and the accumulation of liquidity in the world financial system has most likely succeeded in temporarily forestalling or smoothing the most negative effects of the global crisis of 2008, but it has also led to the creation of a dangerous paradox. The rapid inflation of global financial assets has created new economic bubbles, and there has been no offsetting deflation (no meaningful inflation of general price levels of goods and services). Hence, one could argue that together, these factors—growing the money supply and holding inflation in check—have led to an intrinsic devaluation of money, although because there is no real underlying asset for the value of currency today, this argument is a conceptual one.

Symptoms such as negative interest rates, low levels of inflation despite massively increasing liquidity in the system, and low levels of growth all suggest that the current global financial system may be at the end of its proverbial rope. And the likely continuation of the same strategy—focusing on the creation of even more financial capital that continues to artificially drive up global markets—may actually be quite destructive, especially in the context of simultaneously steeply rising global debt. Consider the analogy of three people riding in an elevator they all believe is going up because the numeric display of floors shows rising numbers, but in truth the display is malfunctioning and the elevator is actually going down. They may feel the drop, but believe more in the rising they see than in the falling they feel, reinforcing one another's beliefs that they are in fact going up because they are essentially comparing their relative performance. But at some point they will hit the ground.

From the fall of the Berlin Wall to the coming fall of Wall Street

Given the collapse of the seven-decade experiment of Soviet Marxism (1917–1989) and the increasing dysfunction of the present dominant model of financial capitalism that began in the 1970s, the question is relevant today whether Milton Friedman's approach (maximizing profit for shareholders) is a natural law or the outcome of an ideology. If it is a natural law, it will continue, even if there are some bumps in the road from time to time. If it is the outcome of an ideology, however, it almost certainly will eventually lose its relevance or be broadly rejected—like any ideology.

The application of Marxism by the Soviet Union to its economy and the economies of its satellites ultimately ended dramatically with the collapse of the Berlin Wall. Financial capitalism, for its part, may end with a similar dramatic collapse of another wall, that of Wall Street, which ironically actually ends at a graveyard where such financial luminaries as Alexander Hamilton, father of the Federal Reserve, and John Jacob Astor, once thought to be the world's richest man, are buried. The imagery of the graveyard is not lost on us. Wall Street derived its name from an actual wall along its eight blocks—first intended to protect early Dutch settlers from the threat of the English and perhaps the Native Americans, but later used to separate "haves" from the "have-nots." Nor should the imagery be lost on those who, like us, sense we have reached a transition point from one form of economy to the next, and see the world still saddled with an old, incomplete model that isn't capable of dealing with the new rules of the game.

Our view is that we may soon need a new, more mutually beneficial and more complete form of capitalism that holistically optimizes value for all three inputs—the people, the planet, the financial capital—to reform the current system of financial capitalism that may one day collapse. Whether a new model is adopted before or as a result of a systemic collapse will be the difference between levels of societal pain, ranging from the tolerably moderate and relatively short, to the severe and long lasting. We still have the ability to choose between these degrees of pain, but maybe not for too much longer.

Different forms of scarcity, yet the same economic model since the early 1970s

As we continued to develop our thinking, we questioned whether the economic model that worked over the last fifty years through the late twentieth century was still appropriate for the twenty-first century. Our argument is that, if economics is the management of scarce resources, there should be a new focus in this new millennium, as the nature of scarcity has also dramatically changed over the last fifty years of Friedman's dominance.

In the 1970s, when the Chicago school of thought emerged, financial capital was scarce but natural resources and labor were not. Friedman's financial capitalism model, therefore, might be considered a logical solution in its time to specifically address this particular form of capital scarcity. This is no longer the case for the world of today. Over the last decade in particular, financial capital has become overly, even dangerously abundant, with negative interest rates no longer a temporary expedient, but becoming accepted in some circles as a possible long-term norm. Meanwhile, other forms of scarcity have appeared in the area of environmental resources (natural capital) and labor, as the advanced skills required for contemporary jobs outpace the training and abilities of those available to work (human capital, social capital).

By way of example, according to the Global Footprint Network (GFN),[3] August 8, 2016, marked the date when humanity exhausted nature's "budget" for that year—every year, this date is moving further back. As the GFN reports, "For the rest of the year [2016], we therefore maintained our ecological deficit by drawing down local resource stocks and accumulating carbon dioxide in the atmosphere. We have been operating in overshoot."

14

Whether this date is accurate or not or whether one ascribes to all that GFN reports, there is an overwhelming consensus that the current economic model takes more from the planet than the planet can now sustainably provide. This is the key motivator for our work on natural capital in the context of promoting greater resource efficiency around inputs. Yet, despite environmental deficits, today's dominant economic model still focuses on creating financial capital (making money with money) at a time when financial capital is overabundant, while ignoring the new forms of scarcity in the early twenty-first century global economy. This situation is simply not a sustainable one, and our view is that a new economic model will inevitably have to emerge—whether it is the one we propose or another—to address these new forms of scarcity and correct the extreme and growing inequality the current system has created. Such inequality is, in part, responsible for fueling various populist movements and societal tensions we are seeing in our communities and on the news almost daily, along with stories of the worsening environmental crisis.

Changes in economic models are the norm, not the exception

Looking even further back in history, we have observed that changes in the prevailing economic model are actually not unusual. They have occurred multiple times in history. And we may be nearing one of these historic transitional moments when the emerging economy with its new rules of the game is going to require a new model.

If we look back to the eighteenth century, value resided primarily in the ownership of land because it was the key resource in the era of the agrarian economy. In the nineteenth and early twentieth centuries, owning the means of production took primacy over land ownership in what was the era of the industrial economy. Over the past fifty years, the focus has been on developing services (mostly financial services) and on creating and accumulating financial capital; this has constituted the era of the service economy. As a result of this focus on generating money, financial capital has now achieved unprecedented levels, suggesting that the task of providing it to the economy has, at the very least, been achieved.

The next economy is likely to focus on what is called "knowledge flow," where value will come from enhancing the capabilities of things and services via knowledge, technology, big data analytics, and the like. Value will reside in the ownership of relationships that enable access to people and knowledge. The recent case of the acquisition by Facebook in 2014 of WhatsApp, a text messaging application now used widely across the globe, may be a sign of things to come and an illustration of the new strategy of the knowledge economy to "focus on connecting the people before aggressively turning them into businesses," as Facebook CEO Mark Zuckerberg said at the time of the acquisition.

Zuckerberg's social network paid a staggering $22 billion in 2014 for the WhatsApp start-up that generated just $10.2 million in 2013. By contrast, in 2008, the company that employs us acquired chewing gum giant Wrigley's for a roughly equal sum, $23 billion, which brought tens of thousands of employees, revenue streams, factories, other infrastructure, globally recognized brands, supply chains, routes-to-market, and more. The comparable costs to Facebook for WhatsApp and to our company for Wrigley's suggests, however, that the market, even in a very imperfect way, is starting to shift to valuing businesses that innovatively build access to people even more perhaps than businesses that generate profits in the shorter term. More importantly, perhaps, is that the comparable acquisition sums suggest that using financial capital metrics alone to comparatively "value" assets of any kind are no longer sufficient on their own and can actually create a distorted or incomplete analytic picture by leaving out the value such acquisitions as WhatsApp can bring in terms of human and social capital.

The opportunity to reactivate and expand the restorative power of business

Every few decades, it's time to rewrite the rules about what generates value for a business, if for no other reason than to ensure such rules for business comport with the "natural" rules of whatever economy we are operating within. And we believe that time is now.

It is increasingly apparent that the managers of the current global financial system are making one last desperate collective attempt, in part through QE initiatives, to maintain the system in its present form, but it is increasingly clear that this is not a viable long-term solution. Major changes are afoot. A new digital and knowledge economy model could burst onto the scene and potentially wipe out the old service business model almost overnight, not unlike how the new car service model Uber disrupted the highly regulated taxi business model, or how Airbnb changed the traditional guest accommodation industry. And there are a staggering number of people rising to join the new middle classes, with Asia adding the economic equivalent of a Germany every 3.5 years and, according to many analysts, having the potential, even with China's slower growth of late, to add the equivalent of three eurozones to the global economy over the next twenty-five years. It should not come as a surprise that such dramatic changes in the world will bring a need for a new model to manage all of the new variables in play.

We may now, in fact, have a once-in-a-lifetime opportunity to reposition business as a restorative power for healing the global economy; an engine for profound positive change for the many. Management science can become a discipline that can create and harvest the true riches of the new century. To achieve this, however, we will need a new model. Not a charity model based on making money one way (often via very aggressive business practices) and spending it another way (via the set up of more corporate foundations). Not a mainstream CSR type of approach based on strategies to mitigate some of the negative impacts of business on the environment and on society through ad hoc (often non-scalable) expensive programs. But rather, it can be a model that leverages the principle of mutuality in business (the sharing of benefits) as a driver of value creation. A model that simultaneously promotes sustainable, profitable business and wider benefits in the form of human, social, and environmental well-being. A model that can mobilize and enhance visible and hidden riches in the many ecosystems in which businesses operate—beyond the legal boundaries of the firm and beyond financial capital. A model that doesn't reject capitalism outright, but rather leverages the power of capitalism, encouraging (not discouraging) the concentration of the different forms of capital not just in the hands of passive shareholders or super-active traders as is the case at present, but rather in the hands of business leaders and entrepreneurs of a new kind who have the talent and sense of broader purpose to bring prosperity to the many rather than to just the few. A model that would be much more complete than Friedman's mono-capital form of capitalism.

Bringing the model to life

Through our research to construct a new multiple-capital business model, we found we had several structural problems. First, the fact that Friedman's model has been so dominant over the operations of nearly every corporation and the curriculum of nearly every business school for much of the last half-century means that the question about whether there is a "right" level of profit for a company has remained an iconoclastic question and a blind spot in the management sciences literature. It has been subsumed, perhaps, by the widespread (mis)assumption that the answer must still be "as much profit as possible," suggesting that any other profit objective has not (yet) entered the consciousness of business.

Second, where the idea of "rightness" with regards to profit has been addressed at all in the literature, it has mostly been framed as part of a greater ideological attack on financial capitalism itself, most commonly from a socialist, Marxist, or environmentalist perspective. Hence, the debate about the possibility of improving the existing model has been more or less stifled by the (mis)assumption that either financial capitalism must be "right" as it is, or it must be "wrong" and should be completely rejected and replaced, and if it cannot be immediately replaced, it should at a minimum be taxed heavily to compensate for some of its dysfunctions. This has not been our approach, accepting or rejecting outright the current form of capitalism, as we appreciate the value and potential inherent in the capitalist model and recognize the importance of concentrating capital in the hands of entrepreneurs. But we question the completeness of the financial capitalism model and the assumptions that underlie the current Friedmanic paradigm that values only a single form of capital (financial), while practically ignoring the importance of nonfinancial forms of capital, along with the need to properly remunerate all stakeholders rather than just the shareholders.

Third, although business has been quite competent at generating and monitoring financial performance, it has a very limited ability with the existing metrics at its disposal to address the riches (value) inherent in individuals, communities, and nature. Without such tools, it is difficult for business to know for certain whether and to what extent it is in the "red" in terms of the holistic value of people and planet. What business is missing are the tools to measure what people and planet, along with profit, each contribute, enable, and destroy across the business ecosystems in which businesses operate.

So, we set out through an ambitious research program to develop a disruptively innovative approach that creates business opportunities by creating social, human, and environmental benefits that correlate with delivering broader performance. To develop a new management theory to decipher how a business can simultaneously promote a sustainable (in terms of longevity), profitable (in terms of financial capital) business and wider benefits (in the form of human, social, and environmental well-being). To develop stable, generic, and actionable nonfinancial metrics for social, human, and natural capital that can drive total business performance across the different forms of capital (including financial), on the assumption that in business, "you only manage what you measure." To leverage these new metrics to assess where there are pain points that can be addressed in the ecosystems in which business operates (across the various forms of capital), and assess what value business operations can add or subtract. And finally, to identify the new business practices that can improve all forms of capital simultaneously, along with a new generation of business leaders willing to operate beyond one form of capital, and a new generation of academics willing to research and teach beyond the one form of capital.

The insights we have uncovered thus far through deep academic research and extensive live business field trials across different geographies and business situations, over the course of almost a decade, are both encouraging and conclusive. The findings to date suggest that a more complete model, not only based on financial performance, can yield higher holistic performance (including financial performance). In other words, "if you don't follow the money, the money follows you." Yes, our piloting—as we will explain in detail in later chapters of this book—is showing how by accounting for and investing in doing social and environmental good, for individuals and communities, growth and earnings for the business can actually be greater than would be the case using traditional profit maximization strategies, all while delivering net increases to individual, community, and environmental well-being that can drive economic performance up.

We realize, of course, that our early findings to date really do fly in the face of the accepted wisdom of traditional business practices and especially of mainstream CSR programs, as they highlight that sustainability-type objectives can be achieved through innovative business models at a profit (rather than purely at a cost), hence, can scale more widely. The findings so far also highlight the fact that the Chicago model is far from the best way to build sustainable prosperity—and may now even pose an obstacle to achieving it. And they show that our new approach has the potential to unleash the restorative power of business to heal some of the wounds it has created.

In making these arguments, we implicitly distinguish ourselves from the supposed efficacy of the purely self-regulating market ideal of Friedman, along with alternatives we perceive to be ways of trying to make a flawed system work more effectively. One such approach is a global tax on capital, as advocated by French economist Thomas Piketty in his best-selling book, Capital in the Twenty-First Century. Despite the undoubted scholarly rigor of its underlying work on wealth inequality, this approach has two major failings in our view. First, it posits a redistribution of wealth while at least implicitly accepting the basic Friedmanic model with all its dysfunction. Second, Piketty's idea of redistribution itself is based on the at best questionable assumption that global institutions or nation-state governments, somehow, will be better equipped than the individual to reallocate taxed value.

As outlined above, the Friedmanic approach is now dysfunctionally growing financial capital, which is already in excess, while Piketty's proposed solution addresses a symptom while implicitly ignoring the root of the economic dysfunction, which is the incompleteness of Friedman's mono-capital model. It is our view that Friedman and Piketty, while indisputably brilliant whether or not one agrees with their propositions, are in their own particular ways fighting yesterday's battles, not today's and tomorrow's, and that we need a new way to address the present forms of scarcity according to the new rules of today's economic game.

The new business model approach that we will describe in some detail in the chapters that follow aims to offer companies and organizations seeking purposeful outcomes the methodological framework, tools, and incentives to help manage the social, human, and natural capital with the same scientific rigor as business (financial) performance is currently managed. The new model's purpose is to grow all the forms of capital simultaneously, rather than just one form of capital—money. It presently consists of a growing number of externally peer-reviewed findings from multiple business and research initiatives across multiple business situations, and now multiple companies, partnering with leading academic institutions from around the world. The findings of our model have, in turn, yielded new metrics that offer those who choose to adopt them a simple, reliable, scalable means—for the first time—to drive business performance and to measure the true impact of business strategies on people and planet. This is true within the company and throughout the business ecosystems in which the business segments operate.

The tools and methods of measurement of our model that begins to complete capitalism enables management to simultaneously deliver profitable business and wider benefits to mankind. They help to distinguish business strategies that deliver social, human, natural, and financial capital from those that do not, or worse, from those that damage these capitals. By employing the new metrics through their strategic plans, business managers will now be able not just to assess impact, as would be the case in a more commonplace CSR type of program, but rather to drive business performance holistically (across all forms of capital and across the ecosystems in which businesses operate). Managers will be equipped with our model to make better informed investment decisions, creating greater transparency and understanding of the positive and negative effects of business decisions.

A very (very) old concept

Surprisingly, perhaps, the new way we are suggesting in this book is actually in many ways a revisiting of an old way of thinking about people, the environment, wealth, and their respective places in the world: the concept of Jubilee.[4] This is the assertion that we need, periodically, to reset the norms to continue to prosper, and to respect a harmonious remuneration system for the key pillars of economic growth—the planet that provides, the people who transform and add value, and the financial capital to ensure the liquidity in the system. At its essence, the Jubilee is about setting the captives free, but practically speaking it is about releasing people from overwork and from over-indebtedness; it is about releasing the planet from overuse and overexploitation; it is about releasing wealth from over-accumulation in the hands of a shrinking minority, many of whom are not equipped to contribute entrepreneurially to growing the wealth currently in their hands in ways that go beyond making financial capital with financial capital.

The rules of the new economy will certainly require a new model to help business entrepreneurs mobilize, accumulate, and manage these new forms of capital that can unlock a broader and more holistically sustainable form of shared prosperity for the world. Today may be such a moment in history to enact the Jubilee in a real, tangible way through a new business model based on its underlying ethical and moral principles. Today may be the time to release the true restorative power of enterprise.

When considering where we are on this journey, we are reminded of the words of the Ecclesiastes, who while referring to a very different situation at a time far in the past, may capture where we are in our own particular timeline:

> *To everything there is a season, and a time for every purpose under the heavens.*

We hope after reading this book you will consider what role you can play—and that you will reflect on what season you and your organization are presently experiencing—in helping to reshape the global economic system along the lines we are proposing. We look forward to you joining us on this journey of discovery and business reformation to help heal the current system that, if left to its own devices, may soon collapse upon itself.

Bruno Roche and Jay Jakub

Chapter 1

The Expanded Meaning of Capital

All truth passes through three stages. First it is ridiculed. Second it is violently opposed. Third it is accepted as being self-evident.

—Arthur Schopenhauer, German philosopher

We can't solve problems by using the same kind of thinking we used when we created them.

—Albert Einstein

When we started our new business model research in 2007, more than a year before the 2008 global economic crisis, our intuition was that the financial capitalism approach of Milton Friedman would soon reach its limits and needed to be reformed and made more complete in order for the economy and business to continue to create value.

The 2008 crisis wake-up call and a growing sense of urgency

In the years since the 2008 crisis, what began as intuition on our part has been dramatically confirmed as fact. The long-accepted (by business) Friedmanic assumption that the sole social responsibility of business is to maximize profit to maximize shareholder value—combined with the pressure of financial capital on business operations and the primacy of short-term financial capital creation over other forms of capital—is viewed by a growing number of stakeholders as being obsolete or no longer fitting for today's economic, social, and environmental context.

Perhaps those who enacted Friedman's views on a wide scale in ways that may have gone beyond his intent were more responsible than the man himself for the distorted form of incomplete capitalism bearing his name that we have today. Friedman's writings, after all, do reflect a recognition that some form of social expenditures are necessary to maximize the long-term profitability of a company. Yet, this seems to have been largely ignored by most who adopted Friedman's model, and the focus—short or long—remains fixed upon maximizing just one form of capital: money. And that is the point that truly matters—acknowledging what Friedman's adherents have done through their single-minded focus on that one form of capital, and what they and others must now accept if capitalism is to become functional and not create even greater dysfunction or be discarded completely for any number of inferior alternatives that could inflict their own dysfunctions on the world.

We are pleased to observe that partly as a result of the wake-up call of the 2008 crisis, there is now a growing and active movement—though still largely disparate and chaotic, made up of a relatively small number of businesses, NGOs, and a handful of academics—that challenges the hypothesis of Chicago. Some of these go by various monikers like conscious capitalism, inclusive capitalism, the triple bottom line, creating shared value, and the B Corp movement. In some instances they even predate the 2008 crisis, like the Social Venture Network, though the magnitude and continuing effects of 2008 helped make the world more open to discussing the current system's shortcomings.

We have no doubt that something good will emerge from this rising awareness. But at the same time, we wonder whether it will be enough—and come quickly enough—to mitigate the most destructive aspects of the pain associated with the economic transition that will come when the current system goes from being dysfunctional to nonfunctioning, as nearly happened in 2008. We don't know the answer to these questions of timing and acceptance, but we feel a strong and growing sense of urgency to share what we have learned about what a more complete form of capitalism could look like, despite the fact that we are still very much on a journey with this work.

Contrary to what happened in 1989 when the Berlin Wall collapsed almost overnight, where the alternative to the Marxist model (the market economy) was already in place in the Western world and ready to take over, the next model that will succeed financial capitalism is not yet in place. Hence, if Wall Street "collapses" in its own way, suddenly like the Berlin Wall did, we don't yet have an accepted alternative to embrace.

The role of global corporations in the development and enactment of a new model

Since business has historically been the driving force that has brought prosperity and taken millions of people out of poverty, and major corporations today have more power than some governments, we asked ourselves, "What would or should be the role and responsibility of large multinational firms in the coming transition from one system to the next?" And we asked how large multinational firms could help give birth to a new, more balanced approach to value creation and value sharing in terms of deploying a new model on a large scale.

Our intuition has been that a model based on the fair sharing of benefits among all stakeholders would create greater, more holistic, measurable value. Such a model, in turn, will necessarily lead to a superior approach for business than the model currently in place most everywhere. But we had to prove it.

Implicit principle needing to be explicit

The business principle that the sharing of benefits across stakeholders could lead to superior business performance over that of maximizing benefits to shareholders has only been implicitly enacted in some successful businesses over the last century or so. But it has not yet been translated into an explicit management theory. It is still more of a selective management philosophy than a scientifically rigorous management methodology that can be more widely deployed. Part of the explanation for this is that prior to the latest crisis, which exposed major underlying weaknesses in the financial capitalism model, most business managers and MBA educators were still too deeply rooted in their belief in the superiority of Friedman's approach to think much beyond it, other than perhaps in relatively narrow, ideological ways. Of course, there are always some exceptions, but none have as yet been simple, scalable, and compelling enough to be transformational.

In 2007, we sensed it was not only possible but also critically important to make this implicit management philosophy more explicit; to translate it into a true management theory. This was because we saw the global economic system as being on the brink of a systemic shift, with most businesses woefully unprepared. Making the implicit more explicit was not going to be easy, as it required developing new metrics for the different forms of nonfinancial capital, along with new management practices, and verifying through rigorous business experiments

28

whether and how this approach can indeed create superior value for all—more than a profit maximization approach. The 2008 crisis brought a welcome new atmosphere of open-mindedness among some business managers and business educators that enabled us to proceed in earnest.

No relationship between profit and growth: a natural law or a worrying outcome of ideology?

To our surprise, our initial research into the management literature highlighted that the questions of "the right level of profit," or whether business should just be about shareholder profit, or whether greater sharing among stakeholders can deliver superior performance over time, have not been addressed rigorously or systematically. With the exception of a handful of papers and case studies, some of which have been only recently published, we found no truly rigorous approach or framework to address this question in a meaningful way.

This space today, again with very few exceptions, essentially constitutes a green field in the literature. This gap in the literature is in and of itself a remarkable circumstance, suggesting a vacuum in economic thinking that underscores the overwhelming influence of the Chicago school, even with all its now obvious dysfunctions becoming more visible to those who look for them. But it is sometimes difficult to see the forest for the trees, especially when our business schools and corporations are nearly all in lockstep in focusing only on trees.

Consequently, we conducted extensive empirical research into the actual performance of more than 3,500 companies (public and private, across different geographies) over roughly a three-decade span (1978–2006) leading up to the kickoff of our business model research program in early 2007. Our purpose was simply to study the causal relationship between profit and growth, i.e., between past profit and future growth, between past growth and future profit, between past growth and future growth, and between past profit and future profit, all over different time scales. The results highlighted a surprising pattern. We found no causal relationship between profit and growth, and no causal relationship between past growth and future growth—regardless of the time scale. The only strong causal relationship we found, in fact, was between past profit and future profit, implying that the only long-lasting pattern in business is its ability to generate profit—irrespective of its top line. A striking and surprising result.

Looking further into a subset of the sample data we examined—focusing on FMCG (fast-moving consumer goods) players (see figure 1)—we highlighted that while growth has been volatile (with ups and downs) over time, profitability during the same time span has steadily and consistently increased. In other words, consistently rising profits have been achieved by thousands of companies over the past few decades in both high- and low-growth scenarios. High profits did not inhibit or promote growth. High-profit businesses, in fact, apparently can live together with sluggish growth. Low growth is sustainable. Low profit, however, is not sustainable. It is remarkable that this pattern held during the 2008 global economic crisis, during which many corporate top lines plummeted while profit continued to increase (though only slightly), hence, securing the continuing remuneration of shareholders whatever the underlying economic context.

These facts appear to validate Friedman's assertion that the only worthwhile goal is to maximize profits, and the role of management, therefore, has implicitly been focused on driving up bottom line net earnings (extracting increasingly more value over time) rather than on managing top line gross revenue, which is

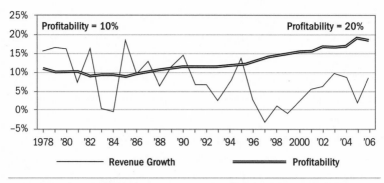

Figure 1. Profitability and growth of the top FMCG companies over a three-decade span.

more prone to external economic fluctuations. One could argue of course that the increased profitability observed across firms over roughly the last thirty years has actually been driven by rising productivity and accelerating technological change. However, the steadily falling labor share[1] in large economies since the 1980s, as pointed out in a recent paper by the Organisation for Economic Co-Operation and Development (OECD) and the International Labour Organization (ILO),[2] suggests the opposite. Over the last three decades, in a majority of large economies, including the United States, Germany, and Japan, wage growth has actually been lagging behind productivity growth, and labor productivity has outpaced real average wage growth.

Furthermore, the steady increase of the so-called "ecological footprint" of human activities reveals that the world now uses the equivalent of at least 1.6 planets to provide the natural resources it needs to operate versus 1.0 planets in 1970, around the time Friedman's model was invented and began to gain more widespread acceptance in business.[3] The productivity gains have not translated into higher remuneration of the planet and the people, but rather have provided greater benefits to shareholders who own the financial capital.

This rather new phenomenon—the lower pre-1970s ecological footprint and the fact that income flowing to labor and financial capital was more or less fixed for decades prior to the dramatic tilt toward the latter in the 1980s—raises a bigger question about whether profit maximization is a natural law or an ideology. And it also begs the question of whether this increase in profitability over time sustains or undermines Friedman's approach, as earlier noted. Being able to outsource jobs to cheaper and cheaper labor markets to help drive the bottom line (net earnings) regardless of top line (gross sales) performance, after all, cannot continue indefinitely. One day there will be no cheaper labor market to which jobs can be outsourced, and the laws of supply and demand will drive up the cost to business of natural resources as the planet becomes more and more depleted. Such is the way of new forms of scarcity that were not present at the birth of Friedman's model.

Figure 1 illustrates that on average, the profitability (bottom line) of the top FMCG companies doubled over the thirty-year period we examined, while revenue growth (top line) was highly cyclical, hence, there is little evidence of any meaningful relationship between the top and bottom lines, only between past and future profit. Thus, it is the Friedmanic ideology, underpinned by management practices and metrics that only drive the bottom line, acting as the profit engine for business—but only for as long as labor and natural resources remain roughly in status quo, which is no longer the case.

Going beyond traditional boundaries and financial capital to measure performance

The need to extend the firm's responsibility beyond its traditional legal boundaries is driven by the fact that most businesses increasingly operate within complex value chains, made of business players of different sizes, operating in different geographies. Metaphorically, one could therefore argue that nowadays each business value chain is only as strong as its weakest link. And responsible, more mutually beneficial business practice is about ensuring that the weakest links of the value chain do not become weaker, but rather are strengthened because the financial cost incurred by a disruption of a value chain is frequently much higher than the cost of maintaining the strength of the weakest players in the value chain. Hence, it is important to embrace the entire business ecosystem in which a business operates, beyond the traditional legal boundaries of the firm. This includes identifying the weakest links and the most acute pain points across all forms of capital, setting up methodologies and metrics to account for them, fostering an environment that is conducive to investing in strengthening those weakest links, and giving them the means to invest and grow (by offering higher margins, as one example among others).

In the same way that economics essentially is the management of scarcity, management is predominantly about measurement. Hence, there is a need to translate the concept of changing various forms of scarcity into the managerial area and to develop new performance metrics for the other forms of capital we discuss in detail in this book (social, human, natural). The idea is to manage the new forms of scarcity and to account for the nonfinancial riches (in nonfinancial ways) that have heretofore been "hidden in plain sight" because of their prior overabundance, yet they have always been critically important for the sustainable performance of any business.

Because the metrics for nonfinancial forms of capital (social, human, natural) have in the context of business application been comparatively weak, confusing, or even nonexistent in some instances, the easiest and most obvious form of capital to measure has been money. This, in turn, has convinced many who are moving into this multi-capital space of research—especially those engaged in management consulting—to simply monetize the other forms of capital in order to deal, eventually, with one metric. This is despite the (obvious to us) fact that monetizing everything may be counterproductive and will certainly be inaccurate, as how can one put a dollar figure on community trust, for example? Or on managers walking the talk of the values they espouse? As we know from history, human nature often follows a path of least resistance, following the logic of Occam's razor, where the simplest explanation or solution is usually superior. In this case, monetizing may seem relatively simple on the surface, but it will be distorting in ways we will later discuss in the chapters on each nonfinancial form of capital.

From the perspective of what constitutes "value" in a business context, the planet provides the resources with which business makes products. The people transform those resources into the actual products and services. The money provides the liquidity to enable people to affect the transformation. This is consistent with the core principles of economic history we noted in the introduction.

The overabundance of money in the system

As stated previously, our argument is that if economics essentially is the management of scarcity, then there is no need to overly focus on financial capital alone because, while money was scarce in the postwar period, this is no longer the case. In fact, if anything, the amount of financial capital that is allegedly currently in existence—we say allegedly because it is inconceivable that much of this financial capital exists as more than a bookkeeping exercise, especially in the case of derivatives valuation[4]—is almost unimaginable.

Since President Richard Nixon moved the US dollar off the gold standard in 1971, financial capital in the form of currency in circulation has been increasing. This occurred rather incrementally through the 1970s until the late 1980s, when the money supply began to grow at a faster rate. Picking up speed in the 1990s, the global money supply started to accelerate in the 2000s, but truly exploded following the 2008 global economic crisis, when developed economy governments simultaneously embarked on a radical expansionary monetary policy that has massively increased the amount of financial liquidity in the global economic system.

As one of many possible examples, through a policy called quantitative easing (QE), the US Federal Reserve has managed via three QE interventions since the 2008 crisis to "purchase" hundreds of billions of dollars in securities in its "open market operations," according to the American Enterprise Institute (AEI) in a 2015 report, "without any real assets, deposits, or money, bringing its total portfolio of securities acquired to $4.236 trillion at year end 2014." By contrast, says AEI, the Federal Reserve's total securities in 2007 were valued at $750 billion. And with the European Central Bank, the Bank of Japan, and the central banks of other leading economies joining the US Fed in doing their own multiple rounds of QE interventions following the 2008 financial crisis, the world is now literally awash in financial capital.

There is plenty of money in the world today, far too much in fact, but the flow of dollars, yen, euros, and pounds have unfortunately been accumulated by just a few in the financial system. This accumulation, in turn, has not translated efficiently into the real economy in terms of job creation, investment, or economic growth, making the gap between those wealthy few and the many poor grow ever wider. This gap has been exacerbated by the fact that the huge QE injections can most easily be absorbed through the financial markets that are dominated by the bigger players, hence, we see a continuing rise of the stock market indexes to breathtaking heights that brings with it a false sense of security for many that the economy must somehow be healthier than it is.

The hidden shortage of other forms of capital

In contrast to the bloated, still growing world money supply, the world's nonfinancial resources (planet in the form of natural capital, and people in the form of human and social capital) are comparatively scarce and becoming more so. When we refer in this context to people, this is not in terms of numbers of workers, since the global population has now grown from about 3.8 billion in 1971 when the dollar ceased to be underpinned by gold, to about 7.4 billion in 2016. Rather, we mean those of working age having the right mix of skills and talent (human capital) and having the right social networks and community (social capital) for the upcoming challenges and the jobs that the new economy will produce and require. And when we speak of planet resources (natural capital), we refer to that which is now being depleted at an accelerating pace and can no longer sustain the current economic growth model. Natural capital is in urgent need of being treated as an increasingly scarce resource, and not as a form of free "renewable riches"—yet it is still essential to ensure a sustainable and healthy future, both for business operations and for mankind at large.

It now makes much more sense to us to change the focus from financial capital onto the management of the nonfinancial pillars of prosperity noted above, rather than continuing to generate excessive financial liquidity while largely ignoring the reality of the new forms of scarcity. To do otherwise would be hazardous. The big challenge we see, however, is mainly psychological in nature in that the paradigm for those who can most easily influence transformational change in the global economy because of where they are placed in that economy has not yet been altered, despite the lessons of 2008. Perhaps there is a sense among many that there is simply too much financial capital to be made to waste time considering the bigger picture. There remains among such elites an abiding impression that if financial capital is just managed more efficiently and maximized for shareholders, the rest of the system will find a way to take care of itself. We do not believe that it will be able to take care of itself, because the rules of the game have changed. The clock is ticking.

The need for new metrics as a foundation for establishing a new management methodology

We need, then, to develop a simple and coherent way to measure the value, impact, and benefits that accrue to the categories of people and planet for business. And we need to find a way for these new metrics—which contribute to defining a more complete form of capitalism—to become part of the management (operating system) of the firm.

We are not advocating a rebalancing or redistribution to overly favor just one of the other forms of capital—as some might advocate and have done so throughout history, with mixed results at best. For example, one alternative noted in our introduction might be to favor people at the expense of the planet and financial capital—the solution Karl Marx advocated and the Soviet Union under Lenin, Stalin, and their successors attempted in a distorted and ultimately very damaging manner. Another approach would be to favor the planet at the expense of financial capital and people, as some today advocate, such as the "degrowth" movement, which wants to downscale production and consumption, and to contract economies, based on the premise that overconsumption lies at the root of long-term environmental stress issues and social inequalities.

We argue that simply skewing the balance in favor of one category of capital at the expense of the other two foundational economic pillars is counterproductive over time. To do so would be a proverbial "half-truth" (a lie), albeit a seductive one since it is easy to say people matter most or that without a restoration of nature we are doomed to global affliction and ultimately to starvation. But it is only when all three pillars of prosperity are balanced—in terms of accounting for what each pillar contributes to the system and how each pillar is remunerated—will prosperity be lasting.

The temptation to do nothing and the imperative to act

Of course, it might be argued that the global economic system will change naturally (self-correct) when it needs to change, therefore, there is no need for man to be proactive. No doubt some people echoed this same "do nothing" refrain prior to the 1789 French Revolution, the 1917 Russian Revolution, the 1929 Wall Street crash, the 1979 Iranian Revolution, the 1989 fall of the Berlin Wall, the 2008 global economic meltdown, and the mass migration crisis affecting Europe and the Middle East that began in 2015, to name just a handful of the upheavals that have afflicted mankind. These transition moments have disrupted whole societies, creating much hardship, the intensity of which was due in large part because societies were unprepared. Perhaps some of the suffering of those periods in our history could have been made far less severe had the proverbial ostriches, heads buried in the sand of denial, been less dominant and therefore change could have taken place before crisis compelled it.

We assert that a new model can and must be evolved right now, and that this can be accomplished from the inside of business by a new generation of enlightened leaders who recognize both the limit of the current system and the potential of the system to be fixed and reoriented to other ends—managers and reformers who want to be empowered to leverage the power of business as a force for good, for a greater purpose, a purpose that inspires.

In the waning years of the former Soviet Union, Mikhail Gorbachev, who knew that the system he was leading was poised to collapse, had the courage to proactively reform and then abandon that system in ways intended to mitigate bloodshed, and he was largely able to do so. One can only imagine the intense and prolonged suffering that could have resulted had not Gorbachev chosen this pathway, with someone in his place choosing instead to use force to impose the collapsing Soviet system beyond its natural end point. Today, there may be many "business Gorbachevs" in the world, whose pro-activeness at this particular moment in history, and whose willingness to expedite transitioning business from the increasingly dysfunctional mono-capitalism of Friedman to a more holistic, complete capitalism such as we envision, could similarly mitigate some of the pain of that transition. But this can occur only if we act quickly, and decisively.

A pragmatic approach

We have worked in senior corporate positions for many years and fully value the positive changes to people's lives that business creates. But the benefits of capitalism need to be expanded and shared for long-lasting, fully functional prosperity to occur for the many. And the failure of the current incomplete capitalist model to incentivize adequate sharing through broader measurement will ultimately (maybe sooner than most think) be its undoing.

We also appreciate the importance of capital concentration, but not in the hands of passive shareholders or for speculation purposes, but rather in the hands of talented entrepreneurs of a new kind who will invest in ways that will produce greater prosperity for all. Our assertion is that since there is the same proportion of entrepreneurs in every population (among the poor as well as the rich), the current system is far from efficiently allocating the capital in the hands of active entrepreneurs. The current mechanism of capital concentration is inefficient in our view and not only leads to unsustainable disparity, but it also prevents active entrepreneurs from accessing capital and leads to destruction of value, such as when useful capital is wasted by passive owners or is fueling financial bubbles instead of being invested in the real economy.

A counterintuitive moral perspective

Rampant inequalities among people constitute a structural reality and may actually not in every instance be inherently unjust, contrary to what many proponents of social justice may believe, but only if a sense of purpose can overcome the dysfunction of greed. This is a counterintuitive way of thinking for many social justice advocates, but one in which lessons for the future economic system can be gleaned.

The crux of our argument is that we all have access to different resources, have different skills, and have different forms of wealth at our disposal, defined not just in financial terms, but also by individual and social well-being, access to abundant natural resources, the gift of public speaking, teaching, of mathematics or science, of dancing, singing, drawing, building, whatever one's special talent may be. Such differences, rather than being viewed as a form of injustice, might actually be better and more accurately viewed as an opportunity. An opportunity for those who have access to something others do not but could benefit from, to be connected with those who have what they may be missing and which they need. In a knowledge economy, where value is inherent not in the accumulation of a single form of capital like money, but rather in building relationships that give one access to the knowledge or other missing ingredients one can use to prosper in different ways, such exchange relationships could be a powerful way to advance social justice without defaulting to redistribution as the only means to do so.

A truly moral system of exchange, however, must be capable of acknowledging and measuring (so that it can be managed in a business sense) the inherent value of different forms of contribution. This would empower each individual involved to maximize the utility of what he or she has received in terms of abilities to fulfill his or her own destiny, while improving the lives of others in the process of pursuing that destiny. In such a context, some concentration of capital in the hands of talented entrepreneurs—in individuals who have the skills to grow whatever forms of capital they are endowed with—is not only a business imperative but can also be a moral act (or at a minimum, not an amoral one) that should be encouraged, as it can be a very efficient way of creating and sharing greater holistic value, playing to the particular strengths of each individual.

Against the backdrop of widening wealth disparity and the injustice of expanding poverty, the notion that prosperity can come from giving more to the one who already has and taking from the one who has less will likely go against the grain for many who are considering it for the first time. But it is not a new concept; far from it. In fact, it is a concept that has been part of the moral foundation of the Western world for several millennia, as illustrated by the ancient parable of the talents or minas (forms of ancient currency, of silver or gold).

In this very old parable, one man was given by his employer five talents (or minas), another two, and a third a single talent to safeguard while the employer was away. The man with five traded for five additional talents, doubling the money he was entrusted with, while the man with two also doubled his money by gaining two more through investment. But the third man, fearing the wrath of his employer, buried his talent to protect it, fearing what would happen if it was lost or squandered, and therefore gained nothing. The third man did, however, earn the rebuke of his returning employer for failing to invest what had been entrusted to him. The parable ends with the third man's talent being confiscated and given to the man who invested the most—the entrepreneur—whose behavior can be interpreted as a form of proactive skillful stewardship of resources. The idleness or lack of effective stewardship by the one who was given the single talent resulted in forfeiture. We are all expected to do our part with what we are given, be this a dollar or a skill, and in an economy that values all forms of capital rather than just one form (money), good stewardship takes on expanded meaning. Hence, financial capital need not necessarily be redistributed evenly to the proactive and idle alike to bring fairness or justice.

This timeless story is very meaningful to us because it goes far beyond narrow ideologies arguing for confiscation and redistribution, or for incentivizing individuals to take and accumulate excessively for their benefit alone. And by so doing, it reveals a narrow pathway to a broader prosperity that can be achieved through leveraging each of our individual gifts, whatever they may be. It illustrates the moral and business principle to give each person, in each generation, the opportunity to prosper, and to concentrate the resources in each generation among those who have the abilities necessary to prosper it.

But this must be done not just for individual gain, but for the greater good, and we will show in this book how applying such an approach can in fact create greater benefits for all, including for the individual contributor who might otherwise focus on squeezing as much profit for himself out of the others. Hence, the pearl of wisdom of King Solomon, whom we quoted in the introduction as having said (in a slightly different form) "one can give freely, but gain more, but another can withhold unduly, yet come to poverty, with the generous person prospering, and whomever refreshes others will be refreshed." These are not just empty words, as we have experimented with this concept and have experienced such outcomes, however unorthodox they may at first appear in the context of the Friedmanic system in place today.

A new methodology for a new paradigm

Given the background above, the first stage of the project we began in 2007 involved identifying the criteria to measure performance/success that puts a premium on relationships, access, and resource efficiency rather than on accumulation of money alone—based on the assumption that the only truly robust set of metrics used today in business are financial performance related. Our research has revealed that while performance measurements for the return on financial capital are robust and effective, the performance measurement of the other two pillars of value creation—planet and people—do exist to some extent, but are currently quite rudimentary, disparate, and not directly actionable in a business model context.

Current planet metrics are rudimentary, focused on external reporting rather than resource efficiency

The planet metrics most used by business, such as carbon footprint or greenhouse gas emissions (GHG), are meant more for external reporting or benchmarking purposes rather than for management action at a business unit level. Companies that emit damaging levels of carbon, after all, have the option under international agreements like the Kyoto Protocol of purchasing carbon credits to at least notionally offset the impact of CO_2 emissions, leaving them free to continue emitting carbon at previous levels if they so choose by paying a relatively small premium for this right. And newer concepts, such as biodiversity offsetting, habitat services, and mitigation banking, to name a few, do not take us much beyond GHG.

Such external-type "output" metrics, in our view, are really aimed at helping a company conform to industry standards for doing "less bad." These metrics also do not have the same level of relevance across industries. For commodities like the manufacture of coffee, for example, measuring carbon footprint is of little use—except perhaps in the case of measuring carbon related solely to transport and distribution. This is because there is actually very little carbon generated in coffee production, including coffee packaging.

By contrast, we are more interested in a business model approach that delivers a management metric or tool for natural capital that can help managers drive greater resource efficiency. Through this enhanced efficiency of inputs rather than focusing just on outputs (footprint), we are seeking to deliver superior business and environmental performance simultaneously. Both the input and output approaches have their uses and are not mutually exclusive by any means, though they have very different purposes and audiences.

While it is an inherently "good thing" to measure and attempt to reduce industrial GHG, CO_2 measurement is not aimed at, nor will it meaningfully directly impact, the resource efficiency of a company. It can be and is used more as a CSR effort or sustainability expense that can do some good in terms of environmental impact. It is also less likely to drive changes in the behavior of business managers beyond that aimed at enhancing corporate reputation, whereas driving managerial behavioral change is the key objective of our new business model agenda. Isolating which of the emissions are most harmful, what is the exact cause, and what can be done about it, moreover, is more difficult to achieve on the grand scale required to have a chance of restoring the environment to good health. GHG strategies are certainly not transformational for business, which is the place that could have more positive impact for the environment than any other if shown how reducing the use of natural resources can create more business value.

For example, we learned from our environmental thought partners and from what we read from other experts who work extensively in the environmental sustainability space that approximately 39,000 gallons of water (147,000 liters) are used in the production of every car made (on average) and 1,800 gallons of water (6,800 liters) are required to grow enough cotton to produce just one pair of blue jeans.[5] Similar statistics can be found for nearly every crop grown and almost every product manufactured. We also learned that intensive farming methods cause soil erosion and land depletion (Australia loses about 500m^2 of farmland every day because of salt rising through the soil),[6] and the world's leading environmental researchers say air pollution is an increasing danger that will bring with it global warming.

We don't dispute any of this and see value in it, though always at a cost, i.e., trading profit for a measure of environmental good, which has no obvious or measurable return on investment for business beyond compliance with government regulation or a more abstract reputational benefit that is very hard to quantify. And without a solid return on investment, can such programs be truly game changing?

Knowing these planet-related statistics and reading about inspirational but mostly anecdotal CSR and environmental sustainability stories published in annual company reports, in our opinion, simply does not provide the necessary leverage for transformational change of business behavior to occur. This is because business managers and their shareholders need more than a simple tradeoff of profit, which they value, for doing some good for others, which they don't value nearly as much. Satisfying government regulators or pressure groups that may be generating bad publicity, or spending a little more on occasion to show shareholders, customers, and consumers that a company is more responsible than the competition, or even because supply chains are no longer secure, are good things, but they are not enough. What businesses really need to be convinced that doing good need not always be a tradeoff for profit, but instead can actually lead to better performance overall, is a robust model that can help them evaluate (at a granular level) what they use and how they use it. This would enable them to make informed decisions and more efficient use of limited resources that can no longer replenish themselves naturally at sufficient rates to compensate for growing resource consumption.

A growing body of knowledge (which we leverage in our model) is developing about the environmental impact of granular (highly detailed) business activities at the business unit level. This is making it possible to run natural capital audits across any supply chain—and to identify the tension points and places where a business can intervene to meaningful effect. We will discuss this approach in detail in chapter 4.

People metrics, disparate and rudimentary, are also more about reporting and benchmarking

A very common type of metric for people at the individual level that we can find in the management literature and in business practices focuses on measuring engagement and well-being at work. The very well-known Gallup Q12 Employee Engagement Survey, for example, covers such broad topics as whether employees know what they are to do and have the necessary means, equipment, and support to do it, or whether they have recently received recognition or praise, indications that they feel cared for, encouraged, or valued. All laudable and interesting proxies to annually test the pulse of the workforce, but in our opinion, basic survey questions such as these comprise an incomplete, and even sometimes misleading proxy for well-being and employee engagement that only lightly scratches the surface of identifying the true drivers of employee workplace well-being.

More importantly, the extent to which companies can be tempted to use this engagement metric as a standalone instrument for employee well-being—because it is simple to administer, and in the absence of anything obvious that is more robust—suggests to us that added metrics are needed to be impactful in ways that can ultimately transform business behavior. A mix of people metrics would enable human resource professionals to craft interventions that will result in a more meaningful impact on employee well-being. This, by extension, can drive greater engagement and with it, better performance, talent attraction, and retention of the best and brightest.

Management metrics vs. reporting metrics

The crux of our argument is that, while it can be useful to have such broad indicators as GHG emissions for the environment— especially for external reporting purposes—and Gallup Q12 engagement scores to check the mood of the workplace from time to time, it is much more practical from a business management perspective to understand the key factors that tend to make production more resource efficient and that tend to increase people's well-being at work and make them happier and more productive, respectively. And we also need to know whether these factors can be qualitatively calibrated across different organizations, countries, and cultures, given the marked variations that often occur across these various boundaries.

External vs. internal business metrics

Broadly speaking, business metrics are either external indicators used for reporting and benchmarking or internal indicators that support management decisions. The former, which speak to the world and include such metrics as NSV (net sales value—i.e., sales less returns, cost of damaged or missing goods, and discounts), cash, earnings, EBITDA (earnings before interest, taxes, depreciation, and amortization—i.e., operating performance absent financing and accounting decisions or tax environments), and GHG (greenhouse gas emissions) are mostly what are called lagging performance indicators. Lagging indicators are mostly about outputs and tend to be fairly simple to measure but hard to impact. They are typically endorsed by external stakeholders, standardized across industries, actionable as an external reporting tool at an aggregated level, and most often communicated via financial and CSR reports.

Internal indicators, by contrast, function mostly as what are called leading performance indicators, which tend to be harder to measure but easier to impact than lagging indicators. Leading indicators speak to the company in its own language, such as through the metrics of ROTA (return on total assets— i.e., the ratio of earnings before interest and taxes against total net assets) and MAC (margin after conversion—i.e., percentage of profit after reducing net sales by prime and conversion costs, showing the relationship between selling price and cost of good). Such internal indicators aim to reflect the distinctive way companies and their like-purposed partners do business (based on culture and values) and support ways of working at the business unit level.

The nonfinancial metrics in the model we propose are of the internal or leading variety, and can be enacted only through a modified business model approach. This makes them potentially transformational for how businesses manage themselves in more mutually beneficial ways for stakeholders. Both leading and lagging types of metrics, however, are required to operate effectively. The nonfinancial metrics are designed essentially to help management do well by doing good, at scale. Or put another way, they are designed to entice business through its self-interest to transition from the narrow objective of maximizing shareholder profit to being global agents for change. Once business is equipped with the tools and practices that will enable it to be profitable by doing good rather than in spite of doing good (or not doing good at all), business leaders can begin to go far beyond Friedman's maxim of the sole social responsibility of business is to maximize shareholder profit and into the realm of revitalizing communities, growing well-being, and restoring the environment on a broad scale.

External metrics are designed to communicate outside the company, but also to compare the company to other players. The model of "completed capitalism" focuses on designing internal metrics that are aligned with a corporation's culture/DNA, can be enacted at the business unit level to help management make sound decisions, and are meaningful to stakeholders across any and every value chain.

Thought-partnering

To begin the process of calibrating the measures that would generate the maximum leverage, we partnered with some of the world's leading thinkers and academic institutions. These included professors from Harvard Business School, Columbia University, Boston University, Stanford, the Paris School of Economics, the Sorbonne, the University of Wisconsin, New York University, the Massachusetts Institute of Technology, the International Institute for Management Development (IMD-Lausanne), the Wuppertal Institute in Germany, Ecole Nationale Supérieure de Statistique et d'Economie Appliquée in Côte d'Ivoire (Ivory Coast), Ateneo de Manila in the Philippines, the University of Indonesia, and Oxford University's Saïd Business School, among others. Our aim was to build on the latest research to identify the key metrics that would help any business in any sector measure its business performance in relation to the way benefits are shared throughout the value chain.

Developing the new model as a non-rival good

Our model for profitable and sustainable operations focused first and foremost on areas of interest to the company that employs us—but we always held in our minds, and explained to our management team, the need for this model to be easily applicable to other companies and sectors, and openly available to all. In our opinion, a mutually beneficial business model would be much more useful to our company if many were operating in a similar manner than if we were a solo act. In the business vernacular, this would be called a "non-rival" or even an "anti-rival" good rather than intellectual property.

A rival good can only be used by one entity, be it an individual or a company. In a business context, it is normally characterized as providing a form of competitive advantage to the user, who seeks to deny its use by others. A non-rival good (or its extended form, called an anti-rival good), by contrast, derives its value from its use by others, not from its exclusivity, hence, a good deemed to be non- or anti-rival must be shared to bring maximum benefits.

An example of a rival good could be a consumable food item, which only really benefits the person eating it, or a tool like a screwdriver that can only be used by one person at a time. A non-rival good, by contrast, could be the Internet, where use by many brings more benefits to each individual user than would be the case if only one person or entity used it in a closed manner. The fact of our new business model being a non-rival or even an anti-rival good is why we took the decision early on—supported by our employers—to openly share what we were learning about how our new metrics and model can drive enhanced performance, measurable across multiple forms of capital in ways that deliver more mutual outcomes for stakeholders in any given value chain.

A model that truly can make more complete what is currently a dysfunctional, incomplete form of capitalism can only be usefully enacted at scale, across many companies and organizations whose shared collective experiences with the approach will grow, refine, and enhance the value of lessons about management practices that deliver mutual benefits. This is why we are now aiming to construct an open collaborative platform approach to the next phase of our work on the model, so that other MNCs—and eventually SMEs (small- and medium-size enterprises), NGOs, foundations, international and academic institutions, and others—can partner with us and with one another within their own particular business ecosystems. In a very mutual way, we can through such a platform share what we have learned to date, and harvest lessons and data from new piloting experiments that will help us all build a more compelling case for a wider rollout of the approach. There is time to keep the proverbial "light under the bushel" when that light provides competitive advantage, and there is a time to take the light out from under the bushel when sharing brings more value. To paraphrase our former CEO, who served as a mentor to us and was a core sponsor of our work, "[your new model] is not about competitive advantage, but to remain competitive in the future, [companies] will have to do this."

We looked at the various parties along the value chain (farmer, supplier, manufacturer, distributor, consumer) and asked how each party was remunerated in terms of the various types of capital we have earlier outlined: human, social, natural, and shared financial. We then determined two broad categories for research: performance metrics that span the various forms of capital beyond just financial, and management practices that can deliver more mutual outcomes for stakeholders in a business value chain.

The performance metrics we developed are based on a set of approximately fifteen variables covering all the forms of capital we address. They have been proven through field-testing to be accurate enough (covering approximately 75 percent of the information—sufficiently robust to be actionable for business), and are thus very stable across business situations. The necessary data will eventually be easily collectable in digital form (e.g., via mobile phones—we are already testing this to good effect in some pilot businesses), replacing the more time-consuming, individually administered surveys we conducted in initial field experiments.

The field survey questions are in a continuous process of recalibration for the many different cultures in which we are operating, and refinement is underway to reduce their number and complexity whenever possible. The questions for human capital cover topics such as working time, work flexibility, job demands, ability to cope, workload, and support from suppliers (in the demand side piloting), customers, fellow program members, and materials and equipment, in addition to income, savings, health care, and housing. Our social capital questions cover topics like affiliation to groups, sources of exclusion, participation in collective actions, trust, norms, behaviors, and attitudes. For natural capital, we focus both on the quantitative (material input per unit of service—MIPS), accounting for all inputs from nature through five metrics (abiotic/biotic materials, air, water use, topsoil erosion) and the qualitative (hot spot analysis), which involves literature reviews, case studies, and input from domain experts. And for shared financial capital, we created what is still a rudimentary (work in progress) "shared value" index that is similar in some ways to the Gini index throughout the value chains we examined in our pilots. Gini measures income distribution in a given country using a number based on individual net income and is used to help explain income disparity. Our shared value index assesses value sharing and identifies hot spots for potential business interventions, develops comparisons across value chains over time, and maps value chains as a framework for further assessment.

The management practices that deliver mutual benefits to multiple stakeholders were calibrated to establish how they developed human, social, and natural capital—with the assumption (later tested through field experiments) that developments in these areas would necessarily have an effect on financial capital. A few examples of mutuality-related management practices we have been testing in live business pilots include a hybrid value system approach (a management concept initially put forward as "Hybrid Value Chain" by Ashoka, a prominent social business network) that consists of partnering with nontraditional (for business) entities, such as NGOs, microfinance lenders, international organizations, and even religious organizations, to leverage their substantial social capital within communities where our business does not operate and has little if any such social capital to use as a market entry point.

Partnering in an HVS essentially is a more mutually beneficial substitute for what would in a more traditional route-to-market initiative be a "cash and carry" type of arrangement whereby the initiating business contracts with distributors to deliver its product to the market for a negotiated fee. An HVS often involves solving the problem of an NGO, a local association, or a local religious organization—for example, in exchange for something like access to the community trust the NGO, the association, or the religious organization has (credibility) that the business cannot just purchase. The NGO in this example might have as its raison d'etre finding meaningful employment for unemployed single mothers in a slum area (a real example), or a religious organization may have among its members a bevy of young, unemployed potential entrepreneurs whom they mentor but who lack the kind of good employment opportunities that the initiating company can bring. An HVS is essentially about mutually beneficial arrangements that are more often than not about far more than exchange of money. As a first step in constructing an HVS, we conduct what we call a business ecosystem mapping exercise, whereby we examine all the likely stakeholders and evaluate their needs to identify the pain points that we can then devise a means to address.

Finding ways to address the needs of the others in the hybrid value system was a means by which we could overcome traditional barriers to entry. Moreover, we are using the local entrepreneur in a new route-to-market type of initiative as the programmatic entry point, rather than something like a product, a sales or profit target, or a philosophical objective such as nutrition, even if nutrition could still be one's desired outcome, as one example. By first empowering the local entrepreneur by ensuring he or she has what they need to be successful, especially the freedom to operate seamlessly within their unique marketplace and culture, we have learned that one may have to go outside the playbook of what business traditionally provides to its value chain stakeholders. This could mean providing an environment conducive to entrepreneurship, such as allowing competitor products to be sold by the entrepreneurs alongside one's own, or being proactive in connecting the entrepreneurs with local relevant players (e.g., microfinance institutions). When we provide these sorts of benefits or flexibility, we are finding that the likelihood of our programs being self-sustaining and scalable is far greater because we are freeing the entrepreneur to be entrepreneurial. If we were instead to relegate the needs of the entrepreneur to a lower tier of importance, as is the case in so many CSR-type social business initiatives we have looked at, we begin to understand why the vast majority of such social businesses fail to earn enough profit to scale up, even if some provide useful benefits for company reputation.

These are just a few examples of many such management practices we are inventing, harvesting from others, and testing in the field. These will grow in number and application over time and through partnerships with other businesses and different types of entities into a second-to-none repository of data and knowledge for enacting a new, more holistic and complete form of capitalism that delivers greater value to all stakeholders. This approach is providing, for the first time, a method of systematically measuring the effects of performance and of management practices across all forms of capital—and in the process is broadening the meaning of the word "capital" itself. The following chapters lay out our approach in more detail for each of these areas of capital, along with case study evidence to support our arguments.

Chapter 2

Five Indicators for Measuring Human Capital and Well-Being at Work

Employees who believe that management is concerned about them as a whole person—not just an employee—are more productive, more satisfied, more fulfilled. Satisfied employees mean satisfied customers, which leads to profitability.

Anne M. Mulcahy, former CEO, Xerox

A good man is one who rejoices in the well-being of others.

Arab proverb

Human capital, as we define it in a business context, involves the many factors that impact individual well-being in the workplace. Simply speaking, greater employee human capital and well-being tends to attract and retain better talent, and happier, more motivated, more talented employees will very likely perform better than those who are unhappy, less motivated, and less talented. It follows, then, that having a sufficiently scientifically robust way of identifying and measuring—in a given corporate culture—the true drivers of employee human capital and well-being can give human resource managers the insights they need to craft interventions aimed at those specific drivers.

To develop a more systematic and granular understanding of individual human capital and well-being at work, we surveyed the literature with our partner Professor Claudia Senik and her team from the Paris School of Economics and established both conventional and unconventional sources to measure it.

Conventional and unconventional sources of human capital and well-being

The conventional sources are those factors that would be part of the work contract and might normally be measured by an organization (e.g., salary, working hours, job location, job description, skills, the type of hierarchy in place and the worker's position in that hierarchy, health risks, and the need for night shifts, among others). However, the literature in social sciences has forcefully established that workers' human capital and well-being extends beyond the traditional conventional factors[1] and includes issues such as the degree of hierarchical steepness in their firm, management style, dispersion of wages, prospects for upward mobility, the corporate identity of the firm, its social responsibility, and relative position in the wage grid of the firm. These unconventional sources are not part of the work contract but have an important role in shaping the overall satisfaction of workers, their human capital and well-being, and their willingness to remain with and contribute to the success of the organization concerned.

We therefore undertook to decipher the unconventional sources of human capital and well-being and have identified four main dimensions. The first dimension includes procedural conditions, or the ways of working. This includes factors such as the management style, whether the company fosters teamwork or individual tasks, the level of autonomy in decision making, the degree of verticality in the organization, relationships one has with his or her line manager, and so on. The second unconventional source consists of social interactions between coworkers, which encompasses the structure and quality of social networks in the workplace, such as how employees are connected to one another, how they interact on issues such as income and wage, comparison and competition, and diversity in terms of age, gender, ethnicity, social class, etc. The third dimension is the corporate identity—what a company stands for, how it behaves and is perceived by others. Corporate identity consists of a shared sense of values, beliefs, and expectations that are often embodied in a specific language. It is an expression of the extent to which managers enact the values they espouse (walking the talk) and can be a powerful instrument to replace more formal and lengthy coordination and decision-making processes. The fourth and final dimension is the social capital among employees that can be described as the habits of trust and cooperative behavior that is built among coworkers.

Well-being at work, human capital, and business performance

While these sources are unconventional, they can be seen as a form of human capital, a firm-specific type of capital of human resources, and can generate significant positive returns in terms of commitment, productivity, and turnover of employees.

Nowadays, an abundant amount of literature has established that these unconventional sources of human capital and well-being have a positive impact on workplace performance and offer the firm a form of competitive advantage. To name a few, Gallup's chief scientist for workplace management and well-being, Jim Harter, and his colleagues have shown for instance that firms listed in the "100 Best Companies to Work for in America" systematically increase more in equity value as compared to the industry benchmark.[2] More recently, other researchers such as Alex Edmans[3] and Petri Böckerman[4] found similar results.

Several reasons explain this phenomenon. Human capital and well-being, for example, tend to promote cooperative behavior and creativity.[5] They help achieve higher performance by creating an environment that motivates people to persist with efforts to attain their goals, to be innovative and take risks. They also help deliver higher productivity because workers who are satisfied and engaged suffer fewer sick days with less absenteeism. Finally, firms with higher human capital and well-being have lower turnover and higher retention rates. There is, therefore, a very compelling business case to create a means to accurately measure human capital and well-being in a firm, to assess their effect, and to manage them intentionally.

Methodology to measure human capital and well-being

One of the critical components of our approach was to formulate a rigorous multistep method for defining and measuring well-being at work and human capital in a replicable manner. This step-by-step process was as follows:

1. Identify the very latest hypotheses, theories, and empirical evidence from the academic literature regarding the unconventional sources of human capital and well-being.

2. Acquire representative samples of human resource data across different representative dimensions of the firm (such as the various geographies in which the firm operates, the various business functions, etc.) that can be generalized, but that also give insights at the level of the individual.

3. Seek through advanced econometric and nonparametric data mining techniques to identify the most relevant and quantifiable drivers in a business context.

4. Reduce the drivers to the greatest extent possible (but not greater) to a small set that can account for the majority of value.

5. Test the stability of the results across different dimensions.

6. Refine the variables until we have metrics that can be effectively measured in a business context.

What we should stress here is that the methodology outlined on the previous pages—assessing the nonconventional variables within the context of any organization—is universal. However, the drivers of well-being at work and human capital are likely to be highly specific to that particular business culture. What follows is an insight into the drivers that were relevant to our company, Mars, Incorporated.

The results presented here are based on representative samples of Mars employees across segments, functions, and geographies. We have covered all continents and segments and surveyed several thousand observations. We used survey data at the individual level, namely the Gallup Q12 surveys as well as ad hoc surveys of employees, both of which were matched with the internal human resource data. We tested numerous variables and discovered a few that were particularly influential at our company.

Scope, data sources, and approach

The core research was conducted based on a representative sample of Mars employees across four different business situations, functions, and geographies. We covered all continents and segments and surveyed about 12,000 observations (individuals × years).

In the first business situation (a relatively small but global and self-contained business unit), we researched and surveyed 100 percent of the employees during a three-year period (2008–2010). For the second and third business situations (much larger and more global business units), we used a representative sample based in multiple countries during a three-year period (2010–2012). For the fourth business situation, we focused on the employees and contract workforce within a single market in Africa (Kenya) during one calendar year (2013). The data sources we used in this work began with the company's Gallup Q12 (twelve generic questions to assess employee engagement) survey answers.

While insufficient as a standalone proxy for human capital and well-being for the reasons we cited earlier (too generic, easily manipulated, ignores context of the drivers of well-being within the specific corporate culture, etc.), the annual Gallup survey does collect a great deal of relevant data. We matched this Gallup Q12 data with internal human resource information at our company covering demographic issues such as age, gender, and family status, and job description in term of salary, division, the employee's line manager, working hours, and similar categories. We developed ad hoc questionnaires with our academic partner from the Paris School of Economics to fill gaps in our data, exploring new dimensions of human capital and well-being like corporate values and identity, knowledge of the "language game" aspect of the company's culture, and attitudes toward sustainability initiatives.

Finally, our methodological approach consisted first of using Gallup results as a proxy for well-being and job satisfaction. Our research team then analyzed the human resource and Gallup data at the individual employee level using data mining and microeconomic analytic techniques to get a precise estimate of the relationship between well-being and its drivers within the culture of the company. We quantified the relationships we discovered between well-being and potential drivers, while controlling for demographics.

Key findings

We identified five drivers that had a disproportionately positive effect on human capital and well-being, organized into two categories: self-centered drivers and firm-centered drivers. The former includes wage and prospect of upward mobility, status (social recognition vis-à-vis others in the company), and organizational features such as the line manager effect. The latter includes corporate identity and employee's social capital.

1. Alignment with corporate identity

The most important factor in being intentional in terms of promoting greater employee human capital and well-being in the workplace is the degree to which an organization's behavior is in line with its corporate identity—does it walk the talk? This falls into two distinct categories.

First, are the corporate vision, identity, culture, and business strategies (especially the sustainability strategies) all aligned? If the answer to this question is yes, then this reinforces a worker's belief in the organization. If they are not aligned with one another, this fact undermines their belief.

Second, are an individual's values aligned with the corporate strategy? In other words, do individual workers share the company's values? If the answer is no, and they do not share the values, the worker will not be fully engaged, however much the organization acts in line with its beliefs and values.

2. Employees' social capital

The second most important element of the five key drivers of human capital and well-being is the level of measurable trust, social cohesion within a community of persons, and that community's capacity to work collectively for the common good, among workers and also between workers and management (teamwork). Social capital is one of the two types of people capital, but it is enacted at a group level, whereas human capital is more about the individual. Nonetheless, social and human capital are closely related to one another, so we tend to survey for both in the business piloting experiments to test the model. We will go into greater detail about how we can measure social capital in the next chapter.

3. POUM (Prospect of Upward Mobility) effect

Our research also demonstrated a significant POUM effect prevails at Mars over an aversion to wage inequalities. Workers accept a greater differentiation of wages within the organization as long as they believe that they can progress upward (a factor linked to the idea of status, below). Upward mobility also has a meaning beyond the idea of promotion, embracing opportunities to learn and to grow as individuals and taking on new responsibilities—factors that can be actively managed by business leaders.

4. Status (social recognition vis-à-vis others in the company)

The fourth major factor, perhaps not unsurprisingly, is that the employee's perception of his or her status vis-à-vis others in the company has a significant symbolic value, regardless of the geographical location. The perceived power, social recognition, and prestige of a role is an important source of human capital and well-being and is likely to create a firm connection between the worker and the employer.

5. Line manager effect

The last main factor affecting human capital and well-being was what we have called the line manager effect. For our purposes, a "line manager" is defined in a business context as the person who manages the individual employee—often called the "direct report" of the line manager, and whose well-being we are measuring. There is clearly the value of a good line manager seeking to support, train, and promote the worker under his or her care. But in addition, changing line managers is significant for human capital and well-being because it endangers the emotional investment a worker has made in that person, and that investment can be significantly eroded when the manager moves. This is not to argue that line managers should not be moved, but rather to say that steps need to be taken to ensure that the new manager has a clear understanding of a worker's past achievements and recognizes them. The research also showed that significantly more human capital and well-being is created in smaller divisions and teams and that length of tenure, not necessarily in the same division, positively impacts human capital.

Overall the importance of human capital and well-being in the success of a business cannot be overestimated. Satisfied and engaged workers are more productive, work better in teams, and are more cooperative with fellow workers and customers. Moreover, being able to say, for example, that a company has been voted as the "best place to work" has a marked effect on equity value.

In other words, building up human capital and well-being, far from being a "soft" subject, is measurable in a stable and scalable way in a business context. Stable, in the sense that the methodology we use to identify the drivers of individual human capital and well-being in a particular cultural context can be used in any cultural context to identify the human capital and well-being drivers that are most relevant for that culture. It can be applied to a business or a government department; an NGO, an international organization, or a foundation. Scalable, in the sense that the methodology can be applied to as large (or small) a workforce as is required, with the same expectation of accuracy of the findings. By effectively managing just five components of human capital and well-being (alignment with corporate identity, employees' social capital, the POUM effect, status, and line manager effect), an organization can enhance its performance and is able to set each key component against a "wage equivalent" for benchmarking purposes (see table 2.1).

Table 2.1 illustrates very simply how the key drivers of well-being at our company—namely corporate identity, social capital, POUM, and status—can potentially equate to an increase in wages. For example, employees who believe their management walks the talk of the values they espouse can (in our company culture, where this trait is highly valued) be considered to be experiencing through enhanced well-being an equivalent of a 30 percent pay increase. Similarly, employees at our company who feel they have a good prospect for upward mobility in their jobs are experiencing the equivalent of an 11 percent pay raise.

Table 2.1 How Wellbeing Drivers Equate to Wage Increases in Mars Cultural Context

Corporate Identity (walk the talk of espoused values)	+30%
Employees' Social Capital	+15%
POUM Effect	+11%
Status	+9%
Line Manager Effect	−2%

Conversely, the impact of a change of line manager on employee human capital and well-being is (on average) the equivalent of the impact of a 2 percent salary decrease.

This exercise is, of course, just for illustrative purposes, as our approach is not meant to be about distilling every form of capital into a monetary equivalent because by doing so, one form of capital could be overvalued vis-à-vis the other forms of capital. Nevertheless, this illustration of how human capital benefits might be monetarily interpreted could help, however imperfectly, the uninitiated begin to connect the dots, so to speak. And it's important to remember that different corporate cultures could have different drivers of employee well-being, and those particular drivers could have different wage equivalencies depending on the nature of that culture. The point of this graphic is simply to reinforce the fact that well-being leads to greater job satisfaction, which, in turn, leads to enhanced performance.

Summary of key human capital well-being findings

❖ **Corporate identity and "walking the talk."** How employees view whether their managers are walking the talk of the values they espouse can be—and is, in our particular corporate setting—a very impactful dynamic on the human capital and well-being of employees.

❖ **Employees' social capital.** Specific "within firm" social capital measured as the level of trust, social cohesion, and capacity to work collectively—and measured between employees and management—is strongly linked to human capital and well-being at work.

❖ **Prospect of upward mobility.** The so-called POUM effect shows that individuals are generally willing to accept a greater differentiation of wages inside their firm as long as they believe they can progress upward in the distribution. The POUM effect prevails in most businesses over the aversion of employees to wage inequalities. Upward mobility can have different meanings, such as vertical or lateral career moves, the opportunity to learn and grow, etc., that can be managed with some intentionality.

❖ **Perceived status matters.** Status—a symbolic value of a job in terms of perceived power and prestige—is a source of human capital and well-being.

❖ **Line manager effect.** Changing a line manager typically has a detrimental effect on human capital and well-being of that manager's direct reports. An engaged, satisfied line manager, conversely, positively impacts the human capital and well-being of his or her direct reports. There is typically more human capital and well-being in smaller divisions and teams, and the tenure of line managers and their direct reports tends to positively impact human capital and well-being.

Chapter 3

Measuring Social Capital— How Communities Affect Growth

A fundamental law of human beings is interdependence. A person is a person through other persons.

Desmond Tutu

A proper community, we should remember also, is a commonwealth: a place, a resource, an economy. It answers the needs, practical as well as social and spiritual, of its members—among them the need to need one another. The answer to the present alignment of political power with wealth is the restoration of the identity of community and economy.

Wendell Berry, The Art of the Commonplace

Just as we plant crops in fertile soil, we want to establish our business in a fertile social environment.

Paul Michaels, former CEO, Mars, Incorporated

Social capital, as we define it in a business context, is expressed at the community level rather than at the individual level, and is the second component, along with human capital, of how we can value people as an asset. Just as human capital provides benefits to business performance when it is at a high enough level, and

69

can drag on performance when it is too low, the "social fertility" of communities—what we call social capital—can also have a positive or negative impact on business performance. As we will explain in this chapter, several business experiments have revealed that social capital is, in fact, a key driver for business and community prosperity and economic performance. Maybe not surprisingly, when there is sufficient trust, social cohesiveness, and capacity to work collectively toward a common end in a given community, such communities have the necessary social fertility to grow and sustain quality of life increases. And greater quality of life of communities, especially in commodity-growing areas that tend to be impoverished, in turn, yields greater economic output, as we will explain.

The question we set for ourselves and for our academic partners (Professor Peter Berger, Boston University, Professor Alain Desdoigts, Paris-Sorbonne University, and their teams) in looking at how to comprehend and then to measure social capital (in a simple, actionable, but accurate way) revolved around the level of impact a particular community had on the success of a business and vice versa. In particular, we wanted to know how much influence a community had on the level of economic output.

How we approached the concept of social capital

Working in a company that is commodities-based and imports a significant proportion of its crops from tropical countries (cocoa and coffee), we were motivated to focus our initial research on small cocoa and coffee farmers. This was in part because farmers of these commodities remain largely impoverished, thereby constituting the weakest link in the value chain and one of the most important pain points in the ecosystem. They are, therefore, beyond just the moral imperative to intervene, because farmers are leaving farming or switching to other crops. This creates powerful business incentives to intervene to increase the supply of commodities such as cocoa because supply projections do not meet demand expectations over the longer term.

The inefficiency of foreign aid in Africa— pouring in money alone does not work

As American economist William Easterly observed in his paper "Can Foreign Aid Buy Growth?", massive international aid has had little impact on economic development in Africa over the last several decades. Despite overseas aid to Africa rising from just over 5 percent of GDP to 17 percent of GDP over the last thirty years of the twentieth century, per capita growth of aid recipient communities fell from around 2 percent per annum to zero (or below zero in the late 1980s and early 1990s). The solution to impoverished farmers in the tropics cannot therefore be found in investing only in traditional proximate sources of growth, such as physical capital (e.g., machines, tools, equipment, technology) or human capital (e.g., education, health).

Armed with this knowledge, we began to consider whether social capital could be the ultimate source and ensure enduring benefits. What we discovered was that the institutional arrangements (mostly informal) in a particular community had a marked effect on the level of investment in machinery, education, or health, which in turn impacted growth. We therefore wanted to understand whether taking into account the social capital dimension and traditionally omitted factors like trust, norms of reciprocity, networks, and forms might have any bearing, and whether there was a method of analyzing how the money invested via international aid might be better invested in the future. This was the starting point of our research, and the very first step was to agree on a definition of what social capital actually is.

What is social capital?
Different definitions[1]

In 1924, the sociologist and anthropologist Marcel Mauss introduced the concept of social capital in his essay, "The Gift: The Form and Reason for Exchange in Archaic Societies."[2] He writes: "Everything intermingles in them, everything constituting the strictly social life of societies that have preceded our own, even those going back to protohistory. In these 'total' social phenomena, as we propose calling them, all kinds of institutions are given expression at one and the same time—religious, judicial, and moral, which relate to both politics and the family; likewise economic ones, which suppose special forms of production and consumption, or rather, of performing total services and of distribution . . ." A highly complicated definition.

In 1986, the sociologist Pierre Bourdieu defined social capital as "the sum of the resources, actual or virtual, that accrue to an individual or a group by virtue of possessing a durable network of more or less institutionalized relationships of mutual acquaintance and recognition [. . .] The volume of social capital possessed by an agent depends in particular on the size of the network of connections the agent can actually mobilise and the volume of capital (economic, cultural or symbolic) personally owned by those with whom the agent is connected."[3]

In 2000, the American philosopher and economist Francis Fukuyama stated that "social capital can be defined simply as an instantiated set of informal values or norms shared among members of a group that permits them to cooperate with one another. If members of the group come to expect that others will behave reliably and honestly, then they will come to trust one another. Trust acts like a lubricant that makes any group or organization run more efficiently."[4] This definition, which was also used by

Professors Steven Durlauf and Marcel Fafchamps, makes it possible to simplify the definition and identify many of the key components structuring social capital (which we will describe later on).

In 1996, within the framework of the growing interest in social capital, the World Bank proceeded to undertake a large-scale qualitative and quantitative data-gathering program in small rural and urban communities in tropical areas, with the objective to develop social capital measurements. The integrated questionnaire initially designed by Ghent University's Christiaan Grootaert and colleagues in 2004 that resulted from this effort[5] has both a qualitative and quantitative dimension, with a questionnaire targeted on households in the surveyed community making a distinction between two forms of social capital: cognitive social capital (inherently subjective) and structural social capital—which we will be calling upon later in this chapter.

Table 3.1 is a succinct summary of some of the most relevant definitions and interpretations of social capital.

As the observations listed under the heading a "club good" (below) would suggest, while social capital has some similarities to financial capital—it can be accumulated, earns a return, can depreciate, and allows you to prevent others from using it—it is also dissimilar in the sense that it cannot be owned or traded. Although there are varying definitions and interpretations, and it has historically been difficult to measure social capital, these descriptions taken together would appear to translate into something like the benefits that accrue to a specific community on the basis of the formal and informal arrangements that community makes for its interactions.

In addition, Nobel laureate Robert Solow noted in 1995 that "if social capital is to be more than a buzzword [. . .] [it] should somehow be measurable even inexactly." Eight years later, effective measurement was still far from a reality, with American

Table 3.1 Summary of the Most Relevant
Social Capital Definitions

World Bank (1990s)	The quality and quantity of a community's social interactions.
Fukuyama (1999) Political Economist, Stanford University	Trust, which acts like a lubricant to make any group run more efficiently.
Fafchamps (2006) Development Economist, Stanford University/ Oxford University	Efficiency of social exchange where formal institutions are weak.
A "Club Good"	Like physical capital, it can be accumulated, earns a return, and requires maintenance because of depreciation.
	Like human capital, it can depreciate with nonuse but not with use. However, it cannot be "owned" by an individual, nor can it be traded.
	It is "non-rival," i.e., if you are using it, other people still can use it.
	It is partly excludable, i.e., you can prevent others from having access to it.
	It yields positive, tangible benefits to members of the "club," e.g., transfers of knowledge and technologies and mutually beneficial collective action.

political economist and Nobel laureate Elinor Ostrom commenting that "social capital [. . .] does exhibit serious problems of measurement." Nevertheless, Ostrom was of the opinion that "it would not be wise at all to dismiss the concept [of social capital utility] on the grounds that it is difficult to measure." That is the issue we sought to address in our new business model program, and we have found a pragmatic way to measure social capital that is proving to be good enough for business and actionable in a business context.

Measurement challenge

One of the main challenges in measuring social capital up to now has been the assumption that it would be too complex to measure for practical use, leaving it to academics to address more theoretically. Because the academic literature suggests there are dozens of variables—upwards of sixty or more, in fact—that together can comprehensively describe a given social capital space, those who might be motivated to use social capital measurement in an applied sense have largely shied away from it, especially in business.

Yet, social capital is noticeable when a high degree of informal support and encouragement is present within a community. And unlike academia, business has the advantage of being able to act on data and findings that are "good enough" rather than only when we are "as close to perfect as we can get," as one would do in engineering or academia, for example. This reality significantly lowers the bar for just how much of the social capital space we truly need to understand to begin drawing reasonable conclusions that enable business to begin taking tangible, impactful actions. The question about social capital for business is how this form of value can be harnessed to drive business growth, while also growing those positive social benefits within communities that make a community more cohesive, collaborative, and resilient.

The answer comes in the form of creating a methodology that combines two types of measurement: qualitative and quantitative. In creating this methodology, we based our approach in part on the basic guidelines laid down by the World Bank (noted in table 3.1 as a measure of the quality and quantity of a community's social interactions), making use of a quantitative social capital survey instrument the bank itself designed but does not appear to have used in any meaningful way we have as yet discovered. We looked to both improve on what the bank started and to qualitatively calibrate the findings from the survey tool using deep anthropological and sociological expertise.

The first measure (qualitative) is rooted in ethnography. We commissioned several teams of anthropologists who were highly skilled and locally very experienced. Our aim was to try to unearth the factors driving social capital to get a baseline for the geographies of our experiments from which we could utilize more business-friendly and simple quantitative survey techniques used in development economics, i.e., those that typically are "good enough" for business in terms of accuracy, but not so academically precise that the time and resources needed to do this would be excessive, making it impractical. The descriptions (qualitative) of the social capital spaces where we experimented were quite involved and also helped us properly calibrate the survey questions we later used to ensure that those surveyed would properly understand our questions and that we would properly understand their answers. For example, in Papua New Guinea we found that among the nine hundred or so dialects spoken in the country, there is not a single word that translates precisely the English word "trust."

The second measure (quantitative) used extensive survey questionnaires (deploying a modified version of the World Bank's Social Capital Assessment Tool). The aim here was to measure the key variables of social capital and the effects of social capital on business success.

To look at the qualitative research in more detail, we interviewed on the supply side coffee farmers in multiple communities in Papua New Guinea and Tanzania, and cocoa farmers in multiple communities in Côte d'Ivoire, with the goal of identi-fying the key markers of social capital. On the demand side, we interviewed micro-distributors in Vietnam, Kenya, and the Phil-ippines. Soon, we will be adding interviews of entrepreneurs in China and India and, on the supply side, of cocoa farmers in Côte d'Ivoire, possibly in Indonesia (Sulawesi), and of coffee farmers in Uganda and possibly in Costa Rica.

We chose Papua New Guinea and Tanzania for the early social capital experiments because they were nearly identical to one another in terms of coffee farmer impoverishment, yet they were very different in terms of culture, language, and geography. And they were also two countries where the sponsoring coffee segment sourced coffee beans. As soon as possible thereafter, we selected Côte d'Ivoire to add a third geography of impoverished farmers, but of a different crop—cocoa, which is core to our busi-ness. And we also selected Vietnam, Kenya, the Philippines, and China soon after to add a new business situation (demand), a new sociological dimension (impoverished urban communities), and new geographies. The purpose was to determine whether social capital measurement could be a diagnostic tool to iden-tify weak points in the distribution channels that could then be addressed through business interventions.

Table 3.2 is a succinct summary of social capital projects undertaken between 2009 and 2015.

Quantitatively, we used the World Bank's Social Capital Assessment Tool (modified and calibrated for our purposes) to isolate factors that could be measured in a replicable fashion and that provided maximum leverage. Broadly speaking, we wanted to be able to identify the degree to which communities relied on formal legal institutions and whether the degree of decentral-ization had an impact. At a more granular level, we wanted to understand the influence of cognitive aspects, like trust, and

Table 3.2. Summary of Our Social Capital Projects, 2009–2015

Business Situation	Countries	Sample Size
Sourcing: Cocoa and coffee farmer communities	Tanzania Papua New Guinea Côte d'Ivoire	2 regions, about 600 households 3 villages, about 500 households First project: 7 villages, about 2,000 households Second project: 5 villages, about 1,200 households
Sales: Small business retailers	Vietnam Kenya Philippines	8 route-to-market areas, from north to south, 2,400 small retailers 6 suburban areas around Nairobi, 450 small business retailers 3 suburban areas around Manila, 400 small business retailers

structural components that include the way the groups are organized (see figure 2).

Breaking these elements down, the cognitive components are more informal and based on expectations of past events: a reliance on being able to trust people to lend and borrow, the reassurance generated by people volunteering and making donations, and the idea that people are not only responsible for their own actions but they will either address their own moral transgressions or their community will hold them informally responsible.

The structural components comprise five elements that focus on the way individuals are accepted or excluded by the group, how involved the community is in decision making, how power is exercised, and how the community is structured demographically.

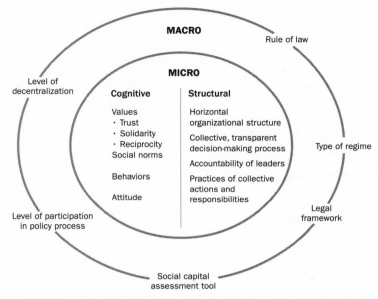

Source: An illustration distilled from the World Bank's 1990 description of its Social Capital Assessment Tool.

Figure 2.   Breaking Down the Elements of Social Capital

The result of this analysis then led us to break these elements into two groups that can be analyzed and measured: behavioral variables and identity variables. The behavioral variables include three of the cognitive components (trust, solidarity, behavior and attitudes) and two of the structural components (exclusion and collective actions).

Table 3.3.   Cognitive Social Capital

Trust	For lending and borrowing
	Expected help from others
Solidarity	Volunteered for charity
	Money donation
Behavior and Attitudes	People responsible for their words and actions
	People remedy their moral transgressions

Table 3.4. Structural Social Capital

Exclusion	Differences leading to exclusion
	Being accepted by the community
Collection Actions	Participation in election campaigns
	Group structures
Horizontal Organizational Density	Group affiliation and structures
Decision-making Process	Top-down (leaders decide)
	Bottom-up (members decide)
Socio-demographics	Gender, age, religion, migration

Key results

What became apparent in the field research and piloting was that social capital was a crucially important driver of prosperity and economic performance—a significant breakthrough discovery. Those communities surveyed that had more social capital performed consistently better economically than communities with less social capital. What's more, after testing more than sixty variables with 7,500 households in thirty-four regions or villages across six countries, we were able to isolate just three variables that explain 75 percent or more of the variations across the social capital space. These are:

1. Social division or cohesion

2. Trust

3. Capacity for collective actions and behavioral attitudes

This discovery suggests a universal nature of mankind in the context of community interaction that is both simple and scalable. Again, this is because the same three variables together consistently account for enough of the social capital space to be practically used in business settings, although the three are weighted differently depending on the situation. By reducing from more than sixty to just three the number of variables businesses can use in any market, culture, or crop, on the supply or demand side—whatever—to decipher, measure, and monitor social capital, what was once considered far too complex for business to use is transformed into an efficient and effective business tool. Such a tool has many possible business uses, most of which are only just beginning to be unearthed and tested.

Where supply is ample, business units can use social capital to determine where enough "social fertility" exists in a supplier community to sustain quality of life increases in that community, so that supply chain partners can prosper alongside the business. In this way, supply chains can become more secure. Similarly, by assessing social capital in advance of a business activity, companies can if they so choose bypass supplier communities where there is insufficient social capital for those communities to flourish as part of the firm's supply chain. When demand for a commodity exceeds available supply, however, the business can choose to intentionally craft business interventions to help grow social capital in supplier communities where it is too low, thereby enhancing the trust, social cohesion, and capacity for collective action that together lead to greater prosperity for all stakeholders.

For example, cocoa farmers in Ghana were engaged by one of our NGO partners, Opportunity International (OI), in a group microlending program that facilitated good agricultural practices (GAP), including application of fertilizer to previously unfertilized cocoa trees. In OI's program, each borrower guaranteed the loans of the other farmers, and this (in the estimation of OI) delivered increased trust, social cohesion, and capacity to work collectively, as the farmers together became more productive by collaborating and sharing the risk. Although OI did not have the means to measure social capital at that time, they shared with us the fact that, with much of the surrounding community watching the farmers in the program prosper, other farmers became more willing to join it and guarantee one another's microloans. This is just one example of how social capital can be intentionally enhanced through a relatively straightforward intervention. Should businesses working with us in the future deploy interventions that could grow social capital, we will seek to measure and track the social capital of recipient communities to understand this dynamic more granularly.

One business leader in our company, when first exposed to our social capital measurement technique, asked if our team could do social capital surveys of communities around sites being considered for new factories. His rationale, based on what he was learning from our team about social capital, was that this could be another important factor to consider, along with cost of land acquisition, access to transportation, electricity costs, tax structure, local infrastructure, and so on, in making the choice of where to put future factories. Another business leader asked if we could assess the impoverished community surrounding one of our factories to determine whether we should invest in growing social capital as a potential means to reverse the surrounding community's decline in quality of life so that it could prosper alongside our facility.

On the demand side, we are using social capital, along with human capital, as a diagnostic tool to help identify pain points (the most pressing needs of others) in distribution that we may be able to address. The poor among our micro-entrepreneur recruits, for example, may not have the financial capital needed to purchase a bicycle with a basket in which they can move our product more efficiently (a real example). By partnering with a microfinance lender, this pain point might be mitigated. Once we have mapped the pain points of the key stakeholders, we can then hold managers and partners—in the pilot businesses used to test the model—accountable for delivering more social (and human) capital rather than focusing first on delivering more sales and revenues. We are finding that more sales and revenues are coming as a result of this counterintuitive approach of putting the needs of the others first, suggesting that if you don't chase the money, the money will find you, as we will illustrate in a specific case study later in this book.

Table 3.5. Social Capital Landscape across Various Pilots

	Social Cohesion	**Trust and Behavior**	**Collective Actions**
Papua New Guinea Coffee farmers 2011	32% (divisions and individualism)	18% (solidarity)	24% (conflicts)
Tanzania Coffee farmers 2011	51%	18% (solidarity)	11% (conflicts and mistrust)
Côte d'Ivoire Cocoa farmers 2012	51% (divisions and individualism)	24%	9% (moral and responsible behaviors)
Vietnam Small retailers 2013	45%	11%	24%
Philippines (Bloom) Small retailers 2015	0%	49%	23%
Kenya (Maua) Small retailers 2015	34%	29%	13%

Note: % indicates proportion of total social capital of 100% explained by specific variable (i.e., the three emerging dimensions—social cohesion, trust and behavior, capacity for collection action—explaining about 75% of the total variance in the survey).

Human capital and social capital

At this point, then, we have isolated eight variables in total that are measurable and impact the economic performance of a business, in addition to being relevant to the communities and individuals involved in the economic activity: three for social capital and five for human capital. The next phase of our work considered whether similar key variables could be isolated in a third area: natural capital.

Summary of key social capital findings

❖ **Social capital has an impact on economic development.** Social capital drives prosperity and economic performance, although it is often ignored and omitted from consideration, possibly due to its perceived complexity or simple ignorance of its significance, e.g., you cannot take a picture of it, like you might a road, school, or well in a typical development project. Like any form of capital, however, social capital can be used, created, and wasted. It can also be intentionally grown through business interventions.

❖ **It is measurable in a stable, scalable way, making it business relevant.** Just three simple component variables—trust, social cohesion, capacity for collective action—account for enough of what constitutes social capital that all of the other variables need not be considered by business, unless of course one is undertaking a purely academic exercise. Social capital, moreover, is stable across varied geographies, and data collection is scalable.

❖ **It is actionable in business operations.** Using social capital, we can assess the fertility of the socioeconomic environment where we and others operate. And we can diagnose and track the impact of targeted actions/interventions by the business.

Chapter 4

Measuring Natural Capital—Making More from Less

Saving our planet, lifting people out of poverty, advancing economic growth ... these are one and the same fight.

Ban Ki-moon, UN Secretary General

The creation is groaning.

Saul of Tarsus, circa AD 50–63

The earth is what we all have in common.

Wendell Berry

The drive to measure natural capital[1] is based upon one simple premise: the earth—despite its capacity for annual renewal—has only limited resources that must be properly valued and managed. In the previous two chapters, we covered how human capital and social capital are related to one another and can be measured in non-monetized ways, bringing value in many different ways, including through their correlation with business performance. Similarly, managing natural capital can also bring business advantages, while also adding to individual and community well-being around the world—a correlation of the capitals that creates a virtuous cycle of measureable benefits.

We will examine in this chapter how businesses can manage their inputs of natural capital with the same level of intentionality and rigor with which they currently measure financial capital. By doing so, they can become much more resource efficient. And we will show how businesses can assess the benefits this new approach can bring not only to the company but to nature and society.

This is not about the much more commonly applied approach—typical in corporate sustainability and other CSR initiatives—to measure outputs, i.e., the ecological footprint of manufacturing, in an effort to do "less bad" to the environment (at a cost) while conforming to external standards, namely CO_2 (carbon) footprint. While both the input and output approaches certainly have their uses, fewer companies today have attempted an inputs-focused resource efficiency approach, which is where we see an opportunity for a "big win" in terms of using natural capital for maximum positive impact in the context of a new, more holistic or complete capitalist business model.

Two broad environmental schools of thought in the literature: inputs vs. outputs approach

The questions we asked ourselves in looking at natural capital were how to make more with less and how the benefits of doing so can be measured. These questions, in turn, have two important implications. First, that a focus must be placed on those factors that can be controlled by the company. Second, that a similar focus must be placed on how the company can optimize the efficient use of natural resources across the entire business value chain, asking how we can measure what we use, and how we can simultaneously increase our economic output.

When we reviewed with our research partner based in Germany—the Wuppertal Institute for Climate, Environment, and Energy—the quite substantial literature on the roots of environmental thinking, what became obvious is that we had a choice between two broad schools of thought that have developed over the last thirty years: In the model, do we focus on controlling inputs or outputs? And which of these approaches would most likely generate the clearest results while driving the most significant and lasting positive change?

The general problem with outputs (purely from a measurement perspective in a business context, rather than one of principle) is that in a highly complex natural environment, it is often difficult to pin down which outputs are the effects of specific causes. Hence, it is harder to manage outputs at a local business unit level. Scientists have managed to find the causal link between CFCs (chloroflourocarbons) and ozone layer degradation, but this was more the exception than the rule with outputs measurement. Outputs are also a measure of what has been already done to the environment, not of what could be achieved. Our view is that business should try to control what is within its purview as early in the manufacturing process as possible, and that this will provide measurable and tangible returns.

We completely agree that it is a fundamental responsibility of business to participate in international and transnational negotiations about limiting outputs, that business should provide governments with the maximum assistance to minimize emissions and harmful effects, and that business should adopt output environmental metrics to report the impact of its activities on the planet. Such agreements and practices, however, tend to be more protracted in terms of time frame and are often beyond the control of a single entity, making them more difficult for business to manage.

The inputs choice

While the outputs approach is appropriate at the aggregate level (i.e., at the corporate and country level), for goal

89

setting, communications, and benchmarking purposes, the inputs approach is more appropriate at the granular, local business unit level to inform management decisions. Our considered business model approach in the area of natural capital, therefore, has been to focus on inputs because they constitute, in our view, the simplest, most pragmatic and actionable approach in a business context for the following reasons:

1. The inputs choice allows for better measurability

Measurability (hence, the ability to manage) decreases along the causal chain from input to impact (output), as illustrated by the model of causal chain analysis developed by the OECD (see figure 3). This is because the inputs into any production system, for example raw materials or fuels, are known in terms of the amount consumed in the production process. However, measuring the effects of the outputs of the production system, for example how particular emissions and effluent mix in the environment to create harm, often cannot be known without detailed and expensive environmental monitoring. As a result, the impacts of some waste and chemicals (e.g., plastics, hormone-mimicking chemicals, etc.) are only beginning to be understood and are currently very difficult to quantify.

2. The inputs choice allows measurement through just five metrics (parsimony)

The inputs approach allows businesses to identify with a great level of accuracy a small range of diverse, but universal, factors (the principle of parsimony, or simplicity)—such as biotic and abiotic materials (i.e., organic and inorganic), water, air, land, biodiversity use—that account for the use of natural capital by a firm. In our experiment described in chapter 7, we were able to isolate just five measures (abiotic/biotic materials, water use,

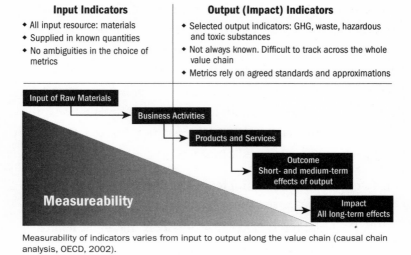

Input Indicators	Output (Impact) Indicators
◆ All input resource: materials ◆ Supplied in known quantities ◆ No ambiguities in the choice of metrics	◆ Selected output indicators: GHG, waste, hazardous and toxic substances ◆ Not always known. Difficult to track across the whole value chain ◆ Metrics rely on agreed standards and approximations

Input of Raw Materials

Business Activities

Products and Services

Outcome
Short- and medium-term effects of output

Measureability

Impact
All long-term effects

Measurability of indicators varies from input to output along the value chain (causal chain analysis, OECD, 2002).

Figure 3.   Inputs vs. Outputs and Measurability of Impacts[2]

air, topsoil erosion) that account through a life cycle analysis for almost 90 percent of the inputs used in the manufacture of the single sachet of coffee that was the subject of the first natural capital experiment. See table 4.1.

It is important to keep in mind, however, that not all of these five universal input metrics are actionable in every business situation. Hence, it is important to focus on those a firm can take action on within its own business context. For example, in

Table 4.1.   The Five Key Metrics of Natural Resource Input

Abiotic	Inorganic materials, e.g., minerals, metals
Biotic	Organic materials, e.g., vegetation, living organisms
Water	Rainfall, spring sources, domestic
Air	Oxygen absorbed through combustion
Topsoil erosion	From, e.g., deforestation, soil salinization

the coffee sachet scenario we describe in chapter 7, we chose to address abiotic materials because they involve nonbiodegradable packaging of a coffee sachet—something very much within the control of the firm. Likewise, we deprioritized the topsoil erosion issue, though if the firm were vertically rather than horizontally integrated, owning its own farming plantations, the topsoil erosion metric would be more actionable and, therefore, more relevant to our specific business.

3. Two simple methodologies can cover almost all of a planet assessment (parsimony)

MIPS (Material Input Per Unit of Services). The input approach enables a business to enact a simple, less labor-intensive, flow-based quantitative methodology (called material input per unit of services, or MIPS). MIPS enables managers to measure all of the five natural capital inputs required to produce one unit of any product (e.g., one cup of coffee). It allows identification of the areas needing improvement and provides benchmarking with other products. As described by Dr. Justus von Geibler and his colleagues from the Wuppertal Institute, "By using MIPS, companies can control the life-cycle-wide environmental pressure potential of the materials they use, their processes, logistics, and products in real time."[3]

HSA (Hot Spot Analysis). The hot spot analysis (HSA) is a qualitative methodology that addresses environmental issues along an entire value chain in a quick and reliable way that cannot be addressed by quantitative approaches (e.g., biodiversity), for which no accurate data exists as yet and that are not satisfactorily covered by input metrics (e.g., waste and emission). It is a methodology based on the work of environmental experts such as Dr. Geibler, knowledge coming from the scientific literature, and existing case studies. The results highlight so-called "hot spots" in a product's value chain (i.e., sections in the value chain where high levels of inputs are being used) that provide a starting point to begin making more with less. Not all hot spots are actionable, of course, but identifying those that are actionable for a firm through business interventions, and then addressing them, could make a firm much more resource efficient.

4. Natural capital productivity ("Factor Four" approach)

The great benefit of the inputs option is that it ultimately offers a greater focus on resource productivity (doing more with less, wasting nothing) that is very aligned with the efficiency principle most companies have adopted to manage their operations. Additional positive features of inputs focus include the possibility to scale and aggregate the information from the smallest to the largest business unit. This is a useful feature for developing an accounting system for the planet, applying the so-called Factor Four framework (see figure 4).[4] Factor Four can help define a single performance ratio measuring the

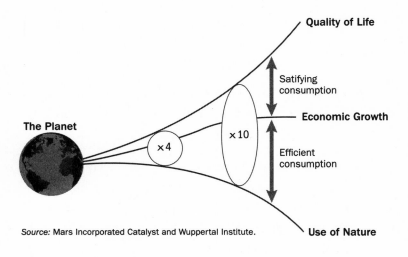

Source: Mars Incorporated Catalyst and Wuppertal Institute.

Figure 4. Factor Four/Factor Ten—Making More from Less

return on input from the planet by comparing the product to the amount of input materials required to produce it through natural resources metrics. And finally, the inputs approach allows fairly simple monitoring of how effectively the planet's resources are being managed over time through a specific business activity.

5. Actionability—Planet accounting system for management purposes

The input approach can ultimately be leveraged to create a four-point planet accounting system (PAS) to measure inputs on a regular basis, comparing inputs year by year, and tracking action taken in strategic areas. The four points of the PAS are as follows:

* **Data inventory.** This section includes database maintenance with all input flows across the product(s) life cycle and ongoing monitoring of the relevant scientific literature to improve the hot spots analysis (HSA).

* **Update.** This involves updating regularly the resource inputs measurements through MIPS and complementing them with the findings of the HSA.

* **Assessment.** This step allows comparison of current results with the last completed measurement in order to assess the real vs. expected impact.

* **Actionability.** We then analyze potential technological improvements to reduce resource inputs and improve resource efficiency in select strategic areas, identifying select potential interventions based on their practicability and environmental impact potential.

6. Inputs and outputs are complementary and serve different purposes

Finally, as illustrated in table 4.2, the inputs and outputs approaches are complementary and connected with one another, but they have different audiences and serve different purposes. While the inputs approach focuses on improving the efficiency of natural resource use and is more appropriate at the microscale of the business unit level for informing management decisions, the outputs approach focuses on measuring and reducing

Table 4.2. Comparison of Input and Output Approaches

	Input Oriented	Output Oriented
Focus	Improve efficiency of natural resources use	Reduce emissions
Metrics	Materials, water, air, land, biodiversity, energy, topsoil erosion	GHG, waste, water
Operating Context	Microscale, business unit level	Macroscale, nation or corporate level
Key Concepts	Factor 4, Factor 10	e.g., "zero emission" target
Purposes	Efficient management of natural resources	Corporate or governmental policies
Outcomes	Eco-innovation: technologies that are more efficient in the use of natural resources input	Global guidelines to reduce the impact on global warming (e.g., eco-taxes, emissions trading system)

waste and is more appropriate at the macroscale of a nation or corporate/industry level for reporting purposes. Hence, the inputs approach in our view is more actionable in a business context—in the sense that it drives management decisions more directly—than is the outputs approach. And when a firm works to improve its efficiency of using natural capital inputs, this also has a positive impact on reducing outputs.

When we implemented the measures outlined in this chapter on one particular example of the "journey of a cup of coffee" from Colombia to the United Kingdom (see chapter 7), we were able to quickly identify where we could achieve economic growth while reducing natural resource use. This presented opportunities to improve quality of life and boost sustainability by using technologies that were already available. In other words, these benefits—both for the planet and for the company—did not require excessive investment in new technology.

This outcome, in turn, suggests that the improvements we found are theoretically available to anyone running any manufacturing business, though in some business activities there may in fact be no available technological solution (as yet), or a technological frontier may not have been reached, creating a time lag while workaround solutions are explored. But we are not seeking here for the perfect solution, but simply to refocus business on what it can do to become more resource efficient on the front end of its activities. And from what we know of our own industry's business ecosystem, there is much room to advance on the inputs side of things. Further, even incremental advances in controlling inputs appear to have big potential payoffs, not just for the initiating business but for the many stakeholders involved.

There is a potential paradox with this approach of "doing more with less to enhance growth," because if taken to an extreme, excessive growth eventually will negate the positive environmental effects through increased resource-intensive business activity. This is known as the Jevons effect or Jevons paradox in economics, when technology enables efficiencies that ultimately drive more rather than less consumption due to increasing demand, so there may be a limit to how resource efficient a company should be, and it may in certain circumstances be important to make less from less for a time to mitigate against resource depletion. That said, business is presently so resource inefficient—in part because natural capital is not yet properly valued and managed intentionally through the kind of measurement we propose—that a great deal of environmental good can be done before any danger point of the Jevons paradox is reached.

What we can claim with growing confidence about natural capital based on our learning to date is that while a purely outputs approach can certainly help a business conform to external benchmarking and reporting standards, an inputs approach in the context of a business model can make us more resource efficient. This is done by giving business managers the hot spot areas/pain points that they may be able to address through new or existing natural capital–related management practices.

Greater resource efficiency, in turn, leads not only to cost savings; we believe it can also promote business growth, with the follow-on effect of reducing the negative footprint we leave behind—all beneficial business outcomes. We have the ability now to collect sufficiently granular data on planet inputs. This gives us a concrete goal: to address the ways in which the use of the five resource areas can be reduced to minimize the impact on the planet while boosting company profitability.

Summary of key natural capital findings

❖ **Natural capital inputs are measurable.** Using five "universal" metrics (abiotic and biotic materials, air, soil erosion, water) and applying a standard value chain life cycle–type analysis, we can acquire the necessary data to measure planet inputs. In the illustrative coffee pilot, these five metrics covered approximately 90 percent of all the input flows across the product life cycle of the pack of single-serve Colombian coffee we examined.

❖ **Natural capital efficiency impacts performance.** Natural capital inputs efficiency can positively impact business performance. Wuppertal's "Factor Four" concept, whereby a sufficient reduction of inputs creates efficiencies that have the combined effect of generating savings, reducing environmental footprint, and driving growth, is very promising. And the simple discovery in the coffee pilot that almost three-quarters of the abiotic materials input metric was covered by the nonbiodegradable aluminum foil packaging gave the business the knowledge it needed to target R&D investment toward developing a biodegradable pack that, in turn, would begin to bring value through efficiency.

Chapter 5

Recalibrating Financial Capital—How Mutuality Drives Profits

We ought to do good to others as simply as a horse runs, a bee makes honey, or a vine bears grapes season after season without thinking of the grapes it has borne.
Marcus Aurelius, Roman emperor, 161–180 AD

If your conduct is determined solely by considerations of profit you will arouse great resentment.
Confucius, Chinese philosopher, 551–479 BC

As yet, we have not analyzed in detail the area of capital about which most people are familiar: financial capital. The key point here is that we wanted to take a fresh look at the way in which capital is generated and, most importantly, how it is shared among the various stakeholders—not only the shareholders and investors, but the various participating parties along the value chain. In manufacturing, for example, every stakeholder adds something of value to what is initially a raw material until it is transformed into a finished product that is then sold to a consumer. In nonmanufacturing enterprises, such as in the services industry, the same questions would be just as relevant, but with value creation and value capture of financial capital occurring across different types of stakeholders.

In essence, we wanted first to gain a detailed understanding of the financial capital generated and captured across the value chain by each key stakeholder. Second, we wanted to develop a simple and scalable approach to understand how financial capital is shared: at the top line level (i.e., where the money goes, the gross sales or revenues) and at the markup level (i.e., how value is distributed across the stakeholders, who each extract some value by adding a cost for their services). Finally, we wanted to develop a system of metrics, in the form of a shared value index, which has some similarities with the Gini index—a measure of statistical dispersion intended to represent the income distribution of a nation's residents. The objective was to assess the distribution of value to the stakeholders, to identify hot spots for attention (where distribution may be overly skewed in a way that squeezes one or more stakeholders too much, thereby creating instabilities), and to develop comparisons across value chains and over time.

We selected coffee as the product category for the very first new business model experiments and analysis on the basis that it is grown in approximately eighty countries worldwide (primarily in the tropics), employs many millions of workers, and is one of the most traded commodities in the world. In addition, 70 percent of coffee worldwide is produced on small family-sized farms and the process is highly labor intensive, making minimal or no use of advanced technology. To provide a meaningful comparison, we based our analysis on the production of one sachet of a single Mars coffee brand and compared the way revenues are shared along the value chain, adjusted for the purchasing power parity[1] (PPP) of each stakeholder.

In addition, we benchmarked the Mars coffee we were examining as a point of comparison against other coffee producers and a variety of different types of crops. What we discovered through this basic analysis of readily available data for the value chain of a single sachet of coffee was that the distribution of revenue was heavily skewed downstream to a surprising degree,

Table 5.1. Shared Financial Capital Analysis of a
Single Sachet of Coffee

Value Chain	Percentage Share (Actuals)	Percentage Share (Purchasing Power)
Distribution	45.0%	37.0%
Manufacturing	39.0%	33.0%
Roaster	4.5%	6.0%
Cooperative	4.5%	8.0%
Farmers	7.0%	16.0%

with 84 percent of the retail value taken by manufacturing and distribution. Even when these figures were adjusted for relative PPP, we found that 70 percent of the revenue was allotted to manufacturing and distribution.

What we should make clear here is that we did not then examine in detail the reasons why revenue is apportioned this way, but we did adjust for the PPP of each stakeholder in the value chain. The next experiment will also adjust for stakeholder investment and risk—a more complex undertaking that will make future findings on shared financial capital more useful to business. Armed with this additional data, it may then be worthwhile to project what might be an ideal distribution of value across the various steps in the value chain. What we wanted to explore initially with this still embryonic shared financial capital experimentation is the sustainability of this situation and the effects of rebalancing how revenue is apportioned. That particular ways of revenue sharing are choices rather than necessities became apparent when we compared other categories.

Whereas the revenue sharing model for coffee is similar to cocoa, it is significantly different from three comparative product categories: sugar, wheat, and car fuel.

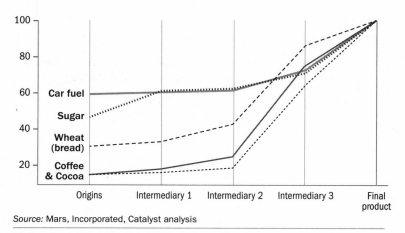

Source: Mars, Incorporated, Catalyst analysis

Figure 5. Basic Comparative Analysis of Coffee Value Chain vs. Other Commodities

What can be seen in figure 5—which does not include any suggestion of what an optimal value distribution should look like, as there is not yet enough data to make such projections—is that there are steep rises between the second and third intermediary value chain stakeholders in the case of both coffee and cocoa. A steep rise does occur at the same phase in wheat, but the percentage share of revenue for the originators of the product (farmers) is 20 percent rather than 7 percent. In the case of sugar, the farmers' share is 40 percent, while for fuel it is 55 percent. As a result, the graph shows a much flatter trajectory in these latter categories, with the intermediaries holding a relatively small share of revenue. The steep curves point to potential areas of tension, which can then be studied in more depth to assess the true level of shared value and how this might be altered through interventions for mutual benefit of more of the stakeholders in the chain, thereby making supply chains more stable.

There are a number of factors that may help explain the shape of the curves in figure 5, including the fact that some commodities benefit from the relative market clout of larger extracting and refining companies while others are typically farmed commodities. This relatively simple exercise to map the distribution of value, however, does get businesses thinking about these matters rather than simply looking for new ways to squeeze supply chain partners in more of a zero-sum fashion—with the corresponding supply chain instability such squeezing can bring when partners are denied their fair share. Part of the explanation for the value distribution variance may be that buyers tend generally to be well organized, at least in comparison with producers (particularly small holder farmers), who are more fragmented. This is especially true in regions where farmers have not organized themselves into cooperatives. Downstream processing of agricultural commodities, moreover, can be quite a complex undertaking, with many variables that we cannot yet assess, and it's important to consider the value of other inputs in creating a final product, such as service and perceived value. Finally, coffee is not an outlier in farm value as a percentage share of retail price, i.e., it is not only true for coffee that there is a sharp increase of the value of the good at the transformation stage.

Our global value chain analysis in the shared financial capital coffee pilot, meanwhile, surfaced a number of issues that we still will need to address through additional business piloting and research as we continue on this journey. For example, at the time of the coffee pilot there was no information available to us about the margins or the profitability of the various businesses along the examined value chain—finding this would require data on input costs that is much harder to secure and verify. We may eventually get there, but we are not currently investing our limited research and experimentation time on this at present. Farmers also tend to be interested in the remuneration of their work, not as much in a value sharing type of proposition, and this likely affects their behavior in ways we do not yet fully appreciate. And we were faced after this pilot with the still unanswered question of whether value at one stage is coming at the expense of value at another stage, i.e., the so-called "cake division" fallacy in game theory whereby taking a larger piece of the whole reduces the amount of cake for the others in a zero-sum way if the others are assumed to equally divide the remaining cake. So, much still remains to be uncovered and will be, but this will take some time.

The upshot of what we did learn on shared financial capital, however, is that using a relatively simple methodology allows any business owner to quickly identify the way that revenues are broadly allocated throughout the value chain and to locate the likely hot spots that may make the system unsustainable or less sustainable in the longer term in the sense that imbalances that do not provide adequate quality of life to a stakeholder could threaten the whole supply chain—which is only as strong as its weakest link. We also learned that virtually all the data used for the analysis already is in the hands of the business units, yet has not to our knowledge—at least in the large and diverse multinational in which we work—been put through this basic analytic lens before this initial pilot. Hence, there is an opportunity for a "quick win" from which new learning can inform better business decision making.

Armed with this information, managers can decide whether they want to intentionally flatten the distribution curves somewhat to make them more stable, as one example. The metrics can then be used to hold submanagers accountable for either delivering such an objective, or switching to supply chains that have a more sustainable value distribution from the outset, when supplier options are more numerous, such as is the case with coffee in our own company because our coffee business is quite modest. Our cocoa business, by comparison, is enormous, and simply switching to other sources of supply is not a viable option for us, so other strategies need to be considered. We are, in fact, about to launch a new pilot among cocoa farmers that will be aimed at making them micro-entrepreneurs, thereby increasing their quality of life in ways we hope will be lasting.

Note here that we are not saying that the system is unsustainable in the short term even with a steep unequal distribution curve. But like all the other areas of capital (human, social, and natural), if the balance is skewed too heavily in favor of particular groups or sectors, then eventually a counter-reaction will occur to try and rebalance the system. Of course, in certain circumstances, such as with a low- or even zero-cost Internet distribution approach, the imperative to change the value distribution may be less applicable than would be the case with commodities-based businesses, so there will always be exceptions.

In the case of cocoa and coffee, one undesirable consequence of the industry's steep remuneration curves is the fact that many farmers are now leaving farming altogether or switching to other crops because their quality of life is too low. This puts pressure on some supply chains and creates incentives for businesses to find ways (quickly) of not only keeping farmers producing these necessary commodities, but also attracting new farmers to meet the growing demand. Raising farmer quality of life, therefore, is becoming an imperative for commodities-based companies like ours, and utilizing the new forms of capital may be able to help advance this objective since many years of international aid investments, mostly in fixed infrastructure in tropical countries, have not moved the needle in this area in ways that are securing commodity supply chains, at least not as yet.

5. Summary of key shared financial capital findings

1. **Measurability.** How financial capital is distributed (shared) among stakeholders in a given value chain is measurable through a shared value index that is generally comparable to a Gini-type index.

2. **Relevance.** By assessing value sharing among stakeholders and identifying hot spots that cause tension or instability in a supply chain, managers can:

❖ make strategic decisions about which supply chains are more or less optimal;

❖ make tactical decisions about what interventions could increase the fairness of value distribution to help stabilize vulnerable supply chains;

❖ hold submanagers accountable for delivering flatter value distribution curves;

❖ develop comparisons across value chains over time.

Value chain mapping for financial capital distribution, moreover, can provide a useful frame for assessment. And by better understanding these distribution curves, business can consider questions such as whether there should be a minimum income at each step—and what that income should optimally be—and whether there should be a maximum standard deviation between the income of each stakeholder, all in a quest to make supply chains more stable and sustainable.

Next steps required

Much work remains to be done on the concept of shared financial capital and calculating the correlation of this form of capital with the others we have covered. Further analysis of the relationship between capital intensity and attributed value must be done. Developing additional case studies that will allow more transparency into value chain mismanagement and its impact on value distribution would be useful, as would qualitative data collection to further understand and support (or refute) the quantitative data already utilized in these early findings.

Chapter 6

Maua—Social and Human Capital: A Case Study

Having described the theory, methodology, and some of the drivers specific to our company, the next step is to show how the process actually worked in field trials. Does our new business model program deliver in practice what it promised in theory? Based on our limited but fast-growing experience, the short answer is yes—and beyond our expectations, as we will explain in this chapter.

In 2013, we launched an exploratory micro-entrepreneurship, micro-distribution pilot business program among impoverished communities in Kenya called Maua with the purpose to test, in a real and especially tough business environment, the hypothesis of our model. In very practical terms, the business objective for Maua was simply to develop a new, profitable "last mile" route-to-market in select urban slum and rural areas of Kenya where our chewing gum business was unable to reach through its traditional route-to-market: namely Nairobi and the rural Kenyan town of Nyeri.

In research terms, the aim of the program was to validate or invalidate the insights of our preliminary analytical hypothesis, assessing whether it is possible to measure, harness, and grow the nonfinancial resources present in poor communities.[1] We were interested specifically in slum dweller social capital and networks, in human capital and knowledge, and in preexisting economic relationships. And we looked to connect these resources with the financial resources that are otherwise scarce, building a business with the objective of solving both a strategic last-mile challenge for the business and a social challenge—the social challenge being to create good jobs and to generate measurable social, human, and financial capital among impoverished communities.

In strategic terms, the intent of Maua was to test—through a pioneering business model experiment based on new performance metrics and unorthodox management practices derived from our approach—whether it is possible to unlock entrepreneurial potential and operate successfully at scale at the so-called base or bottom of the pyramid (BoP) markets. A second goal was to penetrate a hitherto unreachable (for our industry and others) demographic that comprises a huge segment of the population (several billion worldwide) that is expanding rapidly across the less developed and developing world. It is a demographic that is considerably more complex and heterogeneous than the developed markets where most MNCs excel and know how to operate.

Operating successfully at the BoP is a steep challenge for most MNCs, and very few companies have managed over time to scale and earn satisfying returns there, leaving a relatively green field in which to work. If our model worked for a representative sample of this group, such as in the slums of Nairobi, there would indeed be enormous potential for expansion in the coming years, with both manifest business growth potential and deep, lasting social benefits of helping a large segment of the world's population move out of poverty via rewarding work and scalable business models.

The program, therefore, was designed from the outset to create in a synergistic manner both economic opportunities and social benefits for all parties involved, with a focus on addressing poverty and reaching the base of the pyramid markets. Measuring business performance across multiple forms of capital (social, human, shared financial) and across all stakeholders involved was key. And adjusting business strategies to grow these new forms of capital all together leveraged their correlation with economic performance to make the experimental business self-sustaining and scalable, unlike the typical social business that is treated as a cost by the firm rather than an opportunity. In this context, the Maua approach falls within the framework of the vision of renowned management thinker and writer Professor C. K. Prahalad, who believed companies can "do well by doing good." Prahalad argued that the engagement of multinational corporations with those in poverty can produce both profits and positive development outcomes.

Maua, as a side note, is the Swahili word for flower/blossom, and it was chosen because the geographic territories in the slums of Nairobi assigned to each of the Maua micro-entrepreneurs quite literally resembled (on a map) a blossoming flower. The fact that the initiative soon was "blooming" much like a flower in terms of its many positive impacts we will now describe helped the program name resonate more strongly with the surrounding community, a factor that helped to brand it locally and which led us to use variations of the blooming name to brand the Maua-like business initiatives that have followed in the Philippines (Bloom initiative), rural China, and soon India. What we did not know when we launched this first pilot business was how significant the mutual benefits would turn out to be for all of the parties involved when a more mutual approach—stressing the interests of the others, or "the means"—was put at the forefront of the model rather than traditional profit maximization, "the ends."

The context for Maua

The Mars corporation's chewing gum segment, Wrigley's, was the business sponsor and host for the Maua initiative in East Africa. Wrigley's has a chewing gum factory in Kenya and a market share of about 75 percent in the country, but prior to Maua it did not operate in the slum or rural areas assigned to the Maua team. Its main competitor in country has a somewhat lower price point on its gum than the Wrigley's equivalent local brand, but Wrigley's gum offerings in Maua have strong, positive brand recognition in the Maua operating territories. The traditional trade for Wrigley's in Kenya is focused mostly on larger retail outlets, such as supermarkets, as well as smaller outlets such as gasoline stations and drugstores, all working through a master distributor.

By contrast, Maua focuses on a more direct micro-distribution approach via micro-entrepreneurs recruited into the program to move goods by bicycle, for example, from stock points to smaller sellers, such as the kiosks typically found in the lower income areas, along with street vendors, small shops, and some direct sales. Maua is about connecting people with little visible financial capital or the means to earn a living, yet are comparatively rich in human and social capital, with the relatively modest amount of money they need to become micro-entrepreneurs, thereby helping to unlock their potential as their income, well-being, and communities improved. Maua, therefore, was designed specifically to deliver human, social, and financial capital to stakeholders, with the hypothesis that by so doing—focusing on the needs of the others—the company would benefit by breaking into a new demographic. But we wanted to do this in a new way, since we believed the more traditional route-to-market approaches would not work at the base of the pyramid.

Hybrid value system

Rather than rely on the sponsoring firm's local Kenyan master distributor, which had limited financial incentive or capability to distribute gum into the slums or to less populated rural areas, we opted instead to develop a new management practice termed "hybrid value system" (HVS)—a management practice derived in part from the hybrid value chain concept proposed by Ashoka in 2010.[2] The hybrid value chain approach is based on the development of partnerships with a range of nontraditional (for business) citizen-sector organizations (CSOs) to provide social and human capital input through such activities as recruitment and training made possible by the "trust" such CSOs engender in the poorer communities that a typical MNC does not have.

An HVS, defined for our purposes, is an ecosystem that relies on connecting the core assets of several stakeholders. The core business assets Wrigley's contributed included brand recognition, operational capacity, infrastructure, logistics, and reputation. The core intellectual assets of the new business model consisted of its innovative metrics for the different forms of capital, the anticipated correlation among the capitals, a repository of best practices, and access to local universities to collect the data, among others. The core social assets of the partnering CSOs operating in the country included their knowledge of and access to informal social networks, the ability to mobilize them and to provide technical and training support, and their ability to provide micro-finance and efficient electronic forms of payment, such as mobile banking. And the core micro-distribution network comprised a central stock point (the "stockists"), from where two Maua program groups collected goods: micro-distributors (what we call "uplifters"), who would deliver product to smaller retail outlets, and subsistence

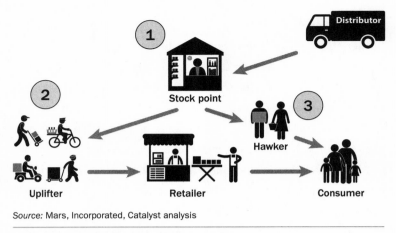

Source: Mars, Incorporated, Catalyst analysis

Figure 6. Basic Maua Route-to-Market

traders (known as "hawkers"), who would sell direct to the customer (see figures 6 and 7).

1. **Stock point.** Receives stocks from the distributor and supplies to the Maua uplifters.

2. **Uplifter.** Receives stocks from stock points and sells door-to-door to retailers.

3. **Hawker.** Receives stocks from stock points and sells to end consumers.

The HVS approach is an efficient, effective way by which institutional voids (pain points) can be addressed, thereby engendering the kind of trust within the community of stakeholders that delivers the social, human, and shared financial capital benefits which, in turn, drive enhanced business performance. Such a counterintuitive approach, however, requires thinking outside the traditional business paradigm and flexing new muscles, so to speak, by partnering with unorthodox entities that business managers simply do not notice, value, or even know how to access, much less how to enlist them in a mutually beneficial business enterprise.

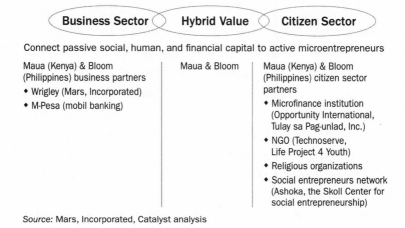

Figure 7. The Hybrid Value System Approach

The challenges this unorthodoxy posed to business managers were many and take time to overcome. NGOs and microfinance lenders, for example, are not motivated by profit, but very often have more altruistic objectives than businesspeople do, and they must be remunerated in ways that address those objectives rather than simply through cash payments for services rendered—the staple of traditional business practice. Such CSO partners—if properly motivated or enticed to collaborate—can connect business to these impoverished communities in a way that businesses typically cannot do on their own, at least in the initial stages. This new type of partnership model, thus, removes a potential major barrier to entry into this space.

Performance measurement

An important competitive advantage for Maua—and for other initiatives based upon the new model we propose—is the rigorous and robust measurement methodology that our team has developed and calibrated with local academic partners. We use the performance measurement and the different forms of capital described in this book, along with the data being collected through regular surveys of program participants and select qualitative interviews run initially by a group of local students (with the plan to collect this data through mobile technology). The focus is on measuring shared financial impact, social capital, and well-being at work—including aspects of human capital, particularly through knowledge exchange and training, as the key performance indicators (KPIs) for the program.

Moving forward through the three years (and counting) of the Maua program, we have observed that the remarkable success of the operation is ultimately built on the particular strengths of the participating local communities. Hence, we decided to eschew sales and revenues targets and instead gave stakeholders (our value chain partners in the distribution business we set up) human and social capital targets. We determined that since the best and perhaps only viable way to build such a business from scratch to break into such a financially impoverished, yet socially vibrant, demographic was to recruit non-traditional (for business) partners, such counterintuitive (for business) targets would be more appropriate and would lead to higher performance. And this hypothesis was proven correct.

Maua start-up

Our decision to try the hybrid value system approach was largely driven by the fact that the social systems within these poorer Maua communities are largely informal. As such, the standard recruitment processes had to be modified. We worked closely with a range of partners mostly in the voluntary sector, drawing on their expertise and knowledge to identify the best people with whom to develop sustainable mutual relationships.

More specifically, we worked initially with select HVS partners to train and equip the micro-entrepreneurs via a custom-designed formal induction process. This comprised a substantive introduction to the program along with advice and guidance on goal setting, business planning, sales and marketing, and recordkeeping. In that regard, as thoroughly described in a 2015 Mars Catalyst—Oxford Saïd Business School teaching case study, a very important Maua partnership was with the NGO Technoserve,[3] which in Kenya focuses on helping women, particularly unemployed single mothers, out of poverty.

We approached Technoserve, in part, because of their deep experience in recruiting and training Kenyan women to be micro-distributors of Coca-Cola products. Technoserve also had relevant experience providing training related to agricultural interventions. Teaming with associates from Wrigley's in Kenya, Technoserve initially helped train 100+ women micro-entrepreneurs for Maua with a low rate of program attrition (approximately 20 percent). These capable partners deployed field officers locally to help oversee and track progress of those they helped train and, together with Wrigley's and Mars University (the company's internal education arm), refined the Maua training regime which Mars University then turned into the Maua Academy to help business managers understand how to operate a Maua model.

By partnering with Technoserve and other NGOs, along with some local religious organizations that were comparatively rich in social capital (trusted by the community), Maua expanded rapidly. We have learned a great deal from partnering with a variety of CSOs on this journey, with some working well, others less so, and we continue to harvest and test new lessons about how to most effectively operate nontraditional partnerships as Maua continues to scale up.

Another fundamental aspect of the Maua program has been the practice of ongoing monthly contact time with the micro-entrepreneurs (two-way communications), partly to offer support, but also to respond to the findings of the Maua team as they explored territory that was new for all involved. This type of routinized sharing experience (which we call "share-out sessions") has proved to be a highly important continual process of learning about what does and doesn't work, adjusting approaches, testing new ideas, learning more, and trying again. The Maua share-out sessions are normally very well attended by program participants and are used for continuing training, mentorship, and awards and incentives; sharing best practices; and offering opportunities to hear from and be inspired by guest speakers.

Share-out sessions actually have many useful aspects. In such meetings, for example, Maua participants might learn how to access microcredit or to connect with those who can sell or rent them affordable bicycles with baskets to more efficiently move their goods. They could get help or advice in such things as setting up savings groups, or being made aware of available health insurance programs. And a key benefit has been fostering meaningful fellowship among Maua participants that is engendering more social and human capital, which in turn is driving more visible teamwork and injecting greater energy and effort—which helps explain the correlative effects of the nonfinancial forms of capital with performance.

Maua's rapid development

Maua entrepreneurs called uplifters essentially move Wrigley's gum (Juicy Fruit, Double Mint, PK, and Big G) from designated stock points (stockists) to kiosks or other micro-sellers in their Maua territories, often on daily credit. The uplifters get a competitive margin that is slightly above that offered by competitive brands, made possible in part by the generally lower overheads of the Maua program vis-à-vis what we would experience in traditional distribution. The uplifters typically pay for the gum in cash (or are themselves granted credit), visiting their network of sellers later in the day to collect what they are owed once the sellers have earned enough to pay. Sales are tracked by Maua field officers, who subsequently provide bonus payouts as warranted. As Maua matured and entrepreneur earnings rose, M-Pesa mobile banking was introduced into the program to make bonus payments more efficient for busy participants.

An important part of the development of the program that cannot be overemphasized has been providing access for the Maua entrepreneurs to financial capital at the micro level through partnering with local microfinance lenders. Lack of financial capital necessary to purchase bicycles or even backpacks to transport Maua product was/is a key business ecosystem pain point that had to be addressed to jump-start the work of program participants who often join the program with minimal financial resources of their own. As the entrepreneurs have flourished, some have been able to upgrade to motorbikes to increase their reach and working efficiency, and some of these, in turn, have started to recruit and equip their own micro-entrepreneurs as a healthy sign of program scaling. And some top Maua performers have begun to transition into managerial roles and even have become small business owners capable of distributing larger quantities of Maua products.

Another highly important practice of the program is that the Maua entrepreneurs are given the freedom to sell other products—even competitor ones—rather than the company compelling them only to sell Maua goods in their baskets as a requirement to be in the program. Hence, the entrepreneurs are unleashed to truly function as entrepreneurs, so we often see Maua baskets including such non-Maua products as cereal, soap, and safe drinking water, along with so-called "aspirational" or nonessential products like chocolates. This entrepreneurial freedom is one of the key reasons why the Maua program has comparatively little attrition to other social types of businesses that seek to exert more control over the route-to-market.

Reflection on design and results

Overall, the package of support offered to Maua participants is designed to empower them to operate in ways that they want to operate (liberating them), while giving them the type of practical support that can more easily be provided by an MNC than by any other type of organization with less practical relevant experience and infrastructure to draw upon. This approach—providing higher margins and more freedom for micro-entrepreneurs, using nontraditional partners from the nonprofit space to gain community entry and to assist in recruitment and facilitate training, and dispensing with sales and profit targets in favor of human and social capital targets—are some of the many ways in which Maua is proving to be a new and distinctive way of doing business.

Having set up the Maua hybrid value system, the obvious questions to ask are how successful has it been in creating value, and how has that value been apportioned across the stakeholder chain? This is not only value in financial terms, but value in the less well-known areas of human and social capital. As illustrated in table 6.1, the answer is that the Maua program has created excellent levels of measurable value across multiple forms of capital.

Since its launch in September 2013 with an initial seven micro-entrepreneurs operating in one slum area (Dandora), Maua has developed across different geographies and has achieved total retail sales exceeding US $7 million, double-digit growth, and excellent profitability. Maua is now representing a significant part of the local Wrigley's business and is managed like a business unit with its own organization.

Table 6.1. Maua Profit and Loss

	Financial Performance		Nonfinancial Performance			
	Retail sales value (in millions USD)	Operating profit	Number of jobs	Human capital	Social capital	Shared financial capital
Year 1 (actuals)	2.9	19%	350	63%	NA	NA
Year 2 (actuals)	4.2	27%	446	76%	+15%	+20%
Year 3 (plan)	5.3	NA	700	80%	+20%	+47%

The performance level of Maua, in fact, has been so notable that it led the leader of the sponsoring business segment to pay the new model an amazingly important compliment. He advised our team that the business would deploy the model whether or not it was intended as a social business because it makes good business sense in and of itself. This is what really separates our model from what one might typically find in the CSR or corporate philanthropy spaces, both of which might be described as "doing good at a cost" in contrast to our holistic capitalism approach of "doing good, and well, at scale"—there are solid business incentives for companies to deploy it, rather than wanting to "look good" (CSR) or to "feel good" (like a corporate foundation).

However, the revenue and retained earnings figures are, in a way, more conventional measures of success. Equally important for the Maua work was being able to measure progress in terms of the way human and social capital appreciated over time. We wanted to measure the benefits to the worker by how equitably the financial capital was shared but also via improvements in education, training, and individual satisfaction. In relation to harnessing and growing social capital, we measured the benefits that accrued to the wider community in terms of job creation and micro-entrepreneurship. In addition, we measured the ways in which any institutional voids were filled: for example, the creation of systems that made it easier to do business and to grow trust in business transactions. The results were also very encouraging in these areas.

Within eighteen months of Maua's launch, the team of entrepreneurs had grown from seven at the start to 450+ people in year 2, on a pathway to 700+ (target plan) by the end of year 3. Maua has delivered excellent levels of measurable value across nonfinancial forms of capital, +13 percent of human capital, +20 percent of social capital, and +20 percent in shared financial capital (a proxy for the financial increase of the micro-entrepreneurs). See table 6.1.

These new micro-entrepreneurs were also drawn from a wide demographic range—youth, parents, and grandparents—and the gender profile was well balanced at roughly 50/50. We also discovered that, when it came to social capital, just three dimensions of this metric (consistent with prior findings testing the metric across various geographies) accounted for 75 percent of the social capital that accrued: (1) social cohesion (willingness to cooperate in group settings) and a mix of (2) trust (faith in the reliability of one another) and (3) collective actions (working together for a common purpose).

There were also correlations (as in earlier experiments) across different types of capital. We found that improvements in social capital and human capital both positively correlated with financial capital—in other words, the more trust there was in the community, and the better trained the micro-entrepreneurs were, the more money the operation made and shared. The benefits accrued for all the parties involved, including the company, which was initially aiming in the piloting phase merely to break even as a way to explore how to deliver more mutual benefits to stakeholders through a new business model approach.

We were also able to measure the fact that the rural operation in Nyeri had a higher level of social capital than the urban operation in Nairobi. This may be due to a number of factors related to differences in who is seen as more or less trustworthy in rural vs. urban settings. For example, rural communities are typically more trusting of fellow townspeople than are urban dwellers because the former have a longer history of living near to one another and, thus, are well known, while the latter tend to be more transient and, therefore, are less well known. Lower-income rural communities also tend to be generally more collaborative because working together may make the difference between eating and going without.

The upshot of designing a new hybrid value system and paying particular attention to the development of and relationship between alternative types of capital (in this case social and human capital) led us to a clear conclusion:

> *When mutuality drives business performance (rather than just narrow profit maximization), greater value is created in terms of individual and community well-being, along with financial profit, both for the sponsoring company's retained earnings and for the micro-entrepreneurs' higher margins.*

Taking Maua to the Philippines

Roughly a year after launching Maua, our team launched a "Maua 2.0" program (Bloom) in the Philippines, beginning in the urban slums of Manila, but involving two business segments rather than just one. The living conditions in the Bloom operating territories, as was also the case in Kenya with Maua, present enormous challenges for businesses to operate under, especially multinationals, and for people to live productive and fulfilling lives. The inhabitants often scrape out a meager living by sorting through trash heaps to garner material for recycling, there is rudimentary sanitation and limited access to clean drinking water, and there are very high levels of unemployment, particularly among young people.

The local team named the Philippines business pilot Bloom—in keeping with the blossoming flower theme of Maua. It operates in much the same hybrid value system way as Maua does (see figure 8).

Encouragingly, we saw the same enthusiasm and commitment in Manila that we had experienced in Nairobi and Nyeri. Within just a few months of launching Bloom, we had established a viable network of more than seventy entrepreneurs who were rapidly building their own network of consumers. And the results were equally encouraging: in its first year the Bloom operation sold several hundred thousand units and contributed

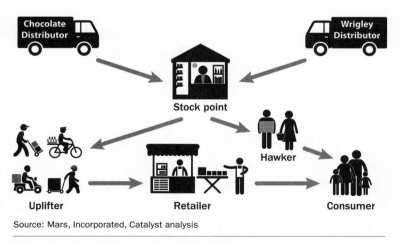

Source: Mars, Incorporated, Catalyst analysis

Figure 8. Basic Schematic of Bloom Program

significantly to profit levels of the two co-sponsoring business segments (Wrigley's and Chocolate) in the Philippines.

Bloom, in fact, has thus far performed along a similar trajectory as Maua in terms of what it is delivering against the same multi-capital key performance indicators, though in a pilot that has added chocolate products to chewing gum and sweets offerings, which meant some additional complexity. As one example, we needed to implement an additional distribution line in Bloom to deliver goods to the initial stock point.

The Maua and Bloom results together have given us an increasing level of confidence that the aforementioned "clear conclusion" about the model is fast becoming a provable fact. And a fact that can help lead businesses to see how they can do both good and well at scale. The business pull for more pilots at the time of this writing is growing fast and is indicative of the convincing nature of the results to date of the Maua and Bloom programs. Our team will soon be launching new supply side pilots in Côte d'Ivoire among cocoa farmers and in Uganda among coffee farmers, and demand side pilots in rural China and India that should add a great deal of new lessons to the mix. While there are the normal bumps in the road in Maua and Bloom that one would expect with any experimental type of entrepreneurial initiative, we are increasingly confident that the model works. It delivers more value in terms of measurable individual well-being, community trust, and social cohesiveness, as well as higher margins for the entrepreneurs, and more profit for the company, all with less investment and overhead than is typical in more orthodox businesses.

All stakeholders benefit in this new approach. Nontraditional partnering stakeholders, such as NGOs and microfinance institutions, are addressing their social objectives through participation and are not being asked by the sponsoring business to adapt to the "cash-and-carry" for "services rendered" type of relationships that typically characterize such business activities. We believe Maua and Bloom, along with the pilots that will soon come on line, can together help prove that what is essentially a mutuality-based business can actually outperform a profit maximization business, not only in the social benefits it creates but in delivering superior revenues and retained earnings. This makes it viable for business, which after all is not about charity.

The big dream

When we first launched Maua, one of our key internal business sponsors at Mars expressed his personal aspiration that the Maua approach, through scaling and replication, could create a million jobs in Africa alone. We were deeply moved by this ambitious vision for the future coming as it did from a seasoned business colleague without the benefit at that time of hard results from a program that was just starting. And while we have a very long way to go to hit that job creation number, we sense that the hard part—developing, refining, testing, and proving that the approach can work and be even more profitable, financially and holistically as we have described, than the old profit maximization default—is now over. Scaling and replication will, of course, take considerable effort, but will likely be more about the "renovation" form of innovation (incrementally improving and growing what exists) rather than the far riskier and more challenging "disruptive" form of innovation (creating a new market and value network) that we believe Maua and Bloom represent. We trust that this million jobs number will one day become a reality.

The game-changing potential

The potentially game-changing nature of this program becomes even clearer when it is compared to alternative strategies that have focused on profit maximization or on CSR approaches.

Some MNCs have also tried to employ what they call "social business" strategies, but most are struggling to make a decent level of profit (or in fact any profit at all). In other words, these alternatives are, for the most part, nice, one-off CSR-type stories rather than replicable, scalable models with the potential to truly transform the way business is conducted. Such CSR-type programs use a mix of metrics solely to measure the impact of what they are seeking to do in ways that generally are favorable to their corporate reputation. Since there are few if any truly global standards for what companies disclose in their annual reports, they can pick and choose which metrics tell the best story for their shareholders and consumers, and we have found very few CSR programs that can deliver measurable enhanced business performance.

In contrast, our new business model uses the heretofore missing nonfinancial metrics of capitalism and uses them not just for impact measurement, but rather to drive greater business performance; holistically, yes, but also financially, all in ways that are measurable and trackable over time. This is because we have discovered that the various forms of capital do indeed correlate with one another. And by taking an HVS partnering approach to construct what are complete businesses based on our new business model, we and our colleagues and partners are truly breaking new ground. We are confident now in stating that the model has proved itself already to be a robust theoretical and practical framework.

We assert that this new model, in fact, has the potential to reform business in-depth once it fully scales up and the "good news" spreads. It has the power to move capitalism closer to completion, and by so doing, can heal a broken world on many levels.

Chapter 7

Coffee–Natural Capital:
Case Study

As discussed in chapter 4, when we employ natural capital—defined as the various natural resources we utilize in the production and distribution process—our focus is on inputs rather than outputs for our new business model experiments. Why? Because we contend that paying attention to the variables that we can directly affect allows us to make measurable improvements quickly by being more resource efficient—which has the dual benefit of making the best use of planetary resources while also delivering bottom line savings. One illustrative example of the way marginal gains can be identified systematically can be found in the pilot study of the inputs required to deliver a single cup of coffee from the farms in Colombia to the consumer in the United Kingdom.

We knew, from prior research carried out by our Wuppertal Institute partners, that differing stages of production and distribution make highly variable demands on the types of resources employed. For example, it was apparent that topsoil erosion and biotic inputs are utilized mainly at the farm level, whereas abiotic, water, and air inputs are utilized across several stages of the life cycle—but weighted toward the point of use. With this broad knowledge, we were then able to refine the research and look in greater detail at four main categories—supply, distribution, manufacturing, and demand—and measure the inputs required at each stage.

On the supply side, we looked at four areas: the agricultural inputs by small-scale coffee farmers in Colombia, the inputs required for primary processing in Colombia, the secondary processing inputs in the UK, and finally the inputs required in the process of packaging production in the UK. On the distribution side, there were two main aspects to consider. The first was transport from the place of origin to the UK, which involved small- to medium-size trucks in Colombia and marine freight. The second set of inputs focused on the primary and secondary logistic hubs in the UK, such as trucks and vans. On the manufacturing side of the coffee business (segment cups), there were three areas where inputs could be measured and adjusted: the UK business site, the packaging of Colombian coffee sachets, and the assembling and disassembling of single-serve coffee machines for recycling and reuse. The fourth and final category was the demand side, where we identified two areas for investigation: the resources used by clients when they consumed coffee, and what we called end-of-life issues involving the disposal of coffee, packaging, cups, stirrers, etc.

The value of this focus is that it enabled us to identify metrics that highlighted not only the percentage of resources used at a specific stage of the product life cycle, but also the physical quantities. For example, it became clear that much of the topsoil erosion happened at the farming stage (see table 7.1).

An example of the new information the methodology revealed is the discovery that a cup of coffee required 3.4 liters of water during its life cycle and that 85 percent of this water was used in the packaging, processing, and drinking stages. In other words, only 15 percent was used at the growing stage. Therefore, focusing attention on minimizing water use at the farming stage would have minimal impact overall, and attention would be better focused on other areas of the life cycle. Not every impact on

Table 7.1. The Journey of a Cup of Coffee (input analysis of a sachet of Colombian coffee)

Metrics	Impact	Percentage of metric	From
Abiotic	146 grams	75%	Packaging, distribution, drinking
Biotic	41 grams	96%	Agriculture
Water	3.4 liters	85%	Packaging, processing, drinking
Air	69 grams	68%	Agriculture, usage
Topsoil erosion	12 grams	100%	Agriculture

every metric is actionable for every business because they typically play in different parts of the ecosystems in which they happen to operate, but the methodology makes it possible to identify and address those that are actionable in ways that improve resource efficiency with multiple positive downstream effects.

This led us to develop the idea of measuring the effectiveness in dealing with what we called hot spots (i.e., environmental issues occurring at each phase of the product life cycle). If addressed systematically, focusing on these areas in the business would enable us to make better use of the inputs. What

Agriculture ⟶ Processing ⟶ Packaging ⟶ Use ⟶ End-of-Life

Source: Mars, Incorporated, Catalyst analysis

Figure 9. Hot Spot Analysis

we discovered was that the three areas where we could make the maximum gains were in agriculture, packaging, and use (drinking).

Next steps for natural capital

The importance of the methodology described in this case study is that it provides a scalable way of expanding the pilot program; in fact, we are now in the process of enlarging the number of natural capital pilots to test its stability across other commodities, such as cocoa. We also intend to enlarge the number of academic partners in follow-on piloting to refine the approach further. During this expansion we will seek to bind the input metrics with specific brands to help create an even more robust and coherent model (for measurement and communication externally). We also have begun to develop a natural capital accounting system with our partners at Oxford University's Saïd Business School; this will help us transfer the methodologies and findings from proof-of-concept to full operational deployment.

This final stage of development, to operational status, will result in us being able to introduce the inputs concept (and the five metrics—abiotic, biotic, water, air, and topsoil erosion) into the broader language of the company and to make the use of natural capital a key focus for the company and for others. The natural capital methodology we outline herein is transferable to other industries because the metrics for natural capital are universal in nature and not specific to the sponsoring company. It is our hope to integrate natural capital accounting into future business pilots that are structured around leveraging human and social capital, to add a further non-monetized driver of enhanced business performance, along with a dimension—nature—that can deliver greater individual and community well-being, along with resource efficiencies that will be valuable to the company.

Chapter 8

Remunerating the New Forms of Capital

For the love of money is the root of all kinds of evil.
Some people, eager for money, have pierced themselves
with many griefs.

Saul of Tarsus

In the previous chapters, we have outlined a number of ways in which it is now possible—for the first time—to define and measure "new" types of nonfinancial capital: specifically, human, social, and natural. We have also shown how a holistic approach that embraces all of these forms of capital can be highly profitable, given the link between them. This, in turn, validates the truth of the ancient principle of wise King Solomon quoted at the beginning of this book:

A man may give freely, and still his wealth will be increased.

Nevertheless, a major question remains unanswered: How are the various forms of capital to be remunerated and what impact will this remuneration have on the notion of the right level of profit? This is a crucial issue because the most obvious and straightforward answer would be to try and monetize them—to convert the benefits of, say, natural capital into financial terms, in the misguided belief that money is the only language business can understand. As the late British playwright

Oscar Wilde once wrote, "We know the price of everything, but the value of nothing." How true.

The temptation of monetization

The assumption by many we have encountered that everything must be monetized is an erroneous one in our view, yet some are beginning to seek answers in the broader "multiple bottom line" space. This common monetization misassumption falls into the Friedmanic trap of seeing business as primarily driven by the maximization of financial profit to benefit shareholders, or in the best case, in a very disproportionate way to stakeholders. After all, one could in theory affix what would be largely arbitrary monetary equivalents to variables like "trust," "prospect of upward mobility," "capacity for collective action," "relationship with one's line manager," "social cohesion," or "walking the talk of espoused values," for example, but what good would this do? And more importantly, how accurate could such figures possibly be? Moreover, would not the monetization of the nonfinancial forms of capital overvalue the relative importance of financial capital in the new knowledge economy, at the expense of properly valuing the other capitals, thereby distorting the whole approach?

The main point of expanding the basket of metrics available to business managers to include nonfinancial forms of capital is to give them tools to manage hitherto unrecognized (squandered) assets available to them. Our view is that this will, in turn, gradually expand their understanding beyond their current financial capital tunnel vision because they will begin to appreciate that human, social, and natural capital actually do have measurable value, are correlated with one another, and can be intentionally mobilized by the business to deliver greater overall performance. In the end, our hope is that there will be a tipping point among business managers where they begin breaking out of the now dysfunctional Friedman paradigm into a new construct that recognizes the true value of people, communities, and natural resources, and their relationship to economic output. Monetizing what cannot be accurately monetized just because the common business language today is all about money is a dangerous trap.

A more complete approach

In stark contrast to the monetizing solution, we argue that, like in nature, where living beings (vegetation, creatures, etc.) are created and reproduce according to their kind, constituting an interconnected ecosystem, the new types of capital need to be remunerated with similar forms of capital—in other words, human for human, social for social, natural for natural. The thought that one form of capital (money) could be used to remunerate the other forms of capital would lead to confusion, in our view, adulterating the role of money. It would also be a form of self-deception, wrongly assuming that the destruction of value in, say, nature, could be entirely compensated for or offset by another, such as money. But before devising specific solutions to the question of remuneration, it is important to consider the three guiding principles behind our thinking about remuneration.

First principle—The Sabbatical

The etymology of the word "sabbatical," reaching back thousands of years via Hebrew (Shabbat / שַׁבָּת), Greek (σαββατικos), and Latin (sabbaticus), indicates its longevity and enduring appeal. In Hebrew, the word Shabbat derives from the Hebrew verb shavat and although it is often translated as "rest," it also indicates a proactive and intentional action (i.e., it is not passive) to abstain from work. The modern Hebrew word for labor strike (shevita, which is related to the verb shavat) refers to the proactive nature of the word to cease work. Shabbat is above all a personal and collective decision.

A form of Shabbat applies to the individual and to communities—one day of rest every week, as an artifact of freedom from the slavery of overwork. According to the Jewish tradition, Shabbat was immediately established after the liberation of the people of Israel from 430 years of slavery in Egypt (where the notion of rest did not exist). It is also the fourth commandment of the Ten Commandments, coming before the commandments not to kill, steal, or bear false witness, and is the only holiday mentioned in the commandments. This notion of proactive rest, as an artifact of freedom from the different forms of slavery, is key in our view in that it illustrates how the concept of Shabbat (proactive rest) is foundational to human freedom. And it can be conceptually enacted as a form of remuneration for people, allowing work to be remunerated according to its "own kind"—for six days of work, there is one day of rest.

Another form of Shabbat applies to nature: one year of rest for the land in every seven years to protect from overuse. During this Sabbath year (also called shmita, literally meaning release), the land is supposed to lie fallow with all agricultural activity forbidden. Whatever agriculture is produced naturally during that year of rest is not meant for the landowner, but rather is for the poor, the stranger, and the beasts of the fields. This is an illustration of how the concept of Shabbat can be enacted as a form of remuneration for the land, allowing nature's work to be remunerated according to its "own kind"—for six years of work, there is one year of rest. Note that during this Sabbath year, all debts between debtors and creditors are supposed to be cancelled and all slaves are to be released.

The final form of Shabbat is the Jubilee and applies to the notion of ownership, property, property rights, and money, i.e., in ancient Hebrew law, the year at the end of seven cycles of seven sabbatical years (shmita)—lasting one year (the fiftieth)—during which all land mortgages were to be returned to the original owners (or their heirs), debt was to be cancelled, and slaves could be released. This is an illustration of how the concept of Shabbat can be used to deal with ownership and accumulation of wealth across generations—which is ultimately linked to the remuneration of ownership in the sense of preventing the over-accumulation of wealth for too long in the hands of a few and that there is an opportunity (for every new generation) to free up the economy, giving all a fresh start—especially those needing a second chance, or to empower those who did not have enough of a chance to start with.

Although we believe these definitions of remuneration and the order in which they are presented (the people, then the land, and finally of ownership) are meant to be interpreted in a broader, perhaps symbolic rather than precisely literal manner, they map across to the four new areas of capital we have been discussing:

1. To individual people on leave (human capital)

2. To communities as a shared period of rest (social capital)

3. To nature, giving it a period to recharge and replenish its resources (natural capital)

4. To allocation of profit (shared financial capital)

In a more literal sense, the sabbatical (whether for a day, month, or year) could enable people, communities, and nature to be restored and reinvigorated, and—importantly—to become more sustainably productive as contributors to society at large. We suggest that offering periods of rest that are purposeful is highly beneficial to business and is ultimately more productive than working resources until they are exhausted, then moving on like a locust would. However, over the course of the last fifty years we have placed less emphasis on the idea of purposeful rest and placed more on Friedmanic profit maximization. We contend that this behavior damages individuals, communities, and nature. It is counterproductive, and humans, communities, and the planet all need periods in which they can recharge and replenish themselves. This is a crucial principle that informs our thinking about how best to remunerate human, social, natural, and financial capital, commensurate with the goal of sustainability.

Second principle—Remunerate on a like-for-like basis

We believe that these new types of capital should be remunerated on a like-for-like basis because monetizing them would be insufficient, problematic, and even distorting.

When we think about remunerating human capital, as one example, it is striking that an important proportion of the most important factors that drive up well-being in the workplace are not financial in nature, but instead relate to such intangible factors as the prospect for upward mobility, social recognition, and the alignment between corporate values and strategies. These factors do relate to financial performance of the individual and his or her employer, but indirectly. Therefore, in order to remunerate human capital, one must develop new business practices, programs, processes, policies, and organizational cultures that will enhance these factors—on top of delivering against conventional sources of individual well-being at work, such as wages, working hours, riskless environments, and the like. This will, of course, include programs of training and development in job-related skills, policies to include opportunities for employees to expand and develop into new areas, provision of time for reflection and creativity and for exposure to new ideas and thinking, and more.

Likewise, if social capital is being remunerated, it is important to remember that there are three general factors that tend to drive up this form of capital—trust, social cohesion, and capacity for collective action. Hence, remunerating social capital in a community requires that "new muscles are flexed" and that we develop new business practices that will include building new networks to connect people further and more meaningfully. These networks should offer new types of contacts and opportunities to leverage for the common good what each brings to the table, not just bringing people together or linking them as an end unto itself, but connecting them with the express purpose of building community. We want to provide opportunities for people to come together in dynamic ways to create innovations that build a better future for all.

When it comes to natural capital, this idea of like-for-like remuneration is even simpler. We can begin by asking how the system can be made better and more efficient as a result of the actions a business can take. Because natural capital measurement essentially comprises five meta variables (water, air, soil, and organic and inorganic material), remunerating it is essentially about ensuring that for every unit of natural capital taken from the planet, a unit of a similar or higher quality is returned to the environment, creating a positive return.

One very simplistic illustrative example of creating a positive natural capital return comes from a coffee-growing operation. After coffee beans are harvested, they need to be cleaned with water before they are dried and processed, and the easiest and most common solution is to wash them in water extracted from a nearby river. The problem this practice can create for the environment is that if the water used to clean the beans is returned untreated back to the river, it can pollute the river because it has been despoiled by the acidity of the coffee beans, creating a negative return on the natural capital for the river and surrounding ecosystem. To address this, the water used for bean cleaning can be treated (cleaned of the acidity) to create a neutral or even a positive return of natural capital (with interest, so to speak) when the treated water—which might now be of a higher quality than when it was initially extracted—is returned to the river. This is provided, of course, that the system used to clean the water does not create too large a footprint of its own.

Third principle—To further decipher and document links between the types of capital

Our research has indeed established promising links between raising the levels of social, human, and natural capital (measured with simple, stable metrics), with an outcome being greater economic performance as measured in financial capital terms. A growing number of pilots have now been completed across several business situations and geographies—with more pilots on the way—that suggest these relationships between the forms of capital are true in different places and situations.

As this methodology continues to develop across industries and business situations, we will develop over time a broad and deep knowledge base comprised of non-monetized and monetized metrics, resulting in new business practices that can deliver greater mutually beneficial outcomes, methodologies, and patterns of relationships between these new forms of capital. By collecting these findings, sharing them openly with like-purposed organizations, and refining the approach, we believe businesses can be equipped with the necessary tools to do business differently, managing different forms of capital and focusing effort on healing the most profound wounds in business ecosystems, all while nurturing healthy financial performance that need not be sacrificed for doing good.

As one might imagine, the obvious aim here is to identify the practices that maximize positive correlations and minimize negative ones. To achieve this, we must not only see these different forms of capital as interdependent—and for that, we need specific measures and reward—but also decipher the natural laws to relate them with one another. This weighing of capitals by what they bring to the equation would help bring real value into the system because we are beginning the process of establishing lasting real value as opposed to wildly fluctuating faux value based purely on perceptions because there is no true underlying value.

Fourth principle—Being intentional and determined to find the "right" level of profit

Determining what is a right level of profit, initially for our company but in ways that can determine what is right for all companies, has from the outset been a key objective of our research.

Today, the right level of profit is largely determined by what the major shareholders want (hedge funds, pension funds, private equity firms, the financial markets, etc.). The right level of profit is imposed from the outside on management through systematic benchmarking (external pressure). It is not emerging from the inside by what the stakeholders need within the firm's business ecosystem to nurture sufficient growth and prosperity (internal pressure). Hence, we assert that to a large extent the level of profit of most firms is not real. Profits tend to either be too high (sometimes extracted in zero-sum ways that can create invisible but disequilibrium effects across value chains that damage stakeholders and the firm itself) or on occasion too low, as what is deemed "right" does not correctly account for the contribution and maintenance of the firm's other forms of capital.

When profits are too high, conventional measures of profits are usually defined net of the cost of maintaining physical capital—plant, machinery, buildings, inventories, etc.—without taking into account the cost of maintaining other forms of capital—human, natural, and social. Such profits may, therefore, be a form of "false" profits in that they constitute a substantial overstatement of the true profit of a firm because they fail to reflect the actual cost of doing business in maintaining these other forms of capital. This tends to artificially increase the level of profit.

Likewise, when profits are too low, conventional measures of profits do not typically take into account the value other forms of capital bring to the business. The conventional management approaches ignore what might be considered the "hidden riches" inherent in the other forms of capital and, therefore, do not know how to harness them for the good of the firm and its stakeholders. This dynamic also tends to artificially decrease the level of true profit.

In a similar vein, not all business ecosystems have the same profile of "brokenness" or of "healthiness" as regards the other forms of capital, yet this is not reflected in the level of profit. One can argue that the more broken an ecosystem is, the lower the level of profit should be, as the more important proportion of the financial value generated by the business should be reinvested to repair the most fragile links in the value chain, or what could be described as the most acute pain points of the stakeholders in any ecosystem. The opposite is also true, that the more healthy an ecosystem, the higher the profit should be.

Some business ecosystems are dysfunctional, not infrequently abysmally so, while others are more healthy as regards their management of nonfinancial forms of capital. Some business ecosystems, for example, are very respectful of the social, human, and natural capital of their environment, while others are truly aggressive—exploiting in a ruthless manner the environment, people, and communities. There are many examples in both categories, and as a result, some business value chains are stronger than others. Since any chain is only as strong as its weakest link, some value chains have more consistently strong links than others, which can be quite vulnerable. The issue is that oftentimes, even within a given business ecosystem, some stakeholders behave in a responsible way, while other behave irresponsibly. Hence, the need to embrace the issue from an ecosystem point of view, not from an individual firm perspective. And, the true value of a business ecosystem is not only in the strength of its individual stakeholders, but in the strength of the links connecting them. This natural law is not reflected yet in existing business practices and performance metrics, and this is precisely the gap that we want to fill.

Based on our still somewhat preliminary, but promising—potentially breakthrough—findings, we are exploring along with our partners from Oxford and elsewhere how to approach the new notion of the right level of profit for a firm. We have chosen to go beyond the conventional notion of profit and the conventional boundaries of the firm, which, in our view, artificially limit the responsibility of the firm. To that end, we introduce the notions of sustainable profit and of mutual profit, and are developing an approach to operationalize these notions.

To illustrate what to many may still seem to be rather abstract concepts, we use examples like the aforementioned one from coffee production, whereby washing the harvested coffee beans pollutes water supplies when the wastewater is reintroduced to the source and can cause environmental damage. Existing measures of profit from coffee are, therefore, not a correct statement of the sustainable level of profit. In evaluating how to restate coffee profits to reflect this one element of mismeasurement, we have looked at alternative technologies for cleaning the water and extracting pollutants, in particular, sugar. This involves investing in equipment and ongoing costs of running that extraction equipment. Together, the cost of capital and the operating costs are the total additional costs of making this part of the value chain more sustainable.

More importantly, however, this exercise also demonstrates the relationship between sustainable and mutual profits because in the process of investing in technology that can extract pollutants from water, the same equipment can be used in other ways to extract sugar from various sources that can, in turn, be converted into ethanol, which can be sold as a source of energy. Such dual-use investments not only can service a positive natural capital function for the firm, but can also in theory create a new revenue stream to offset the cost of treating water contaminated in a coffee-cleaning operation in a way that not only returns natural capital back to the environment, but does so at a profit rather than a financial capital deficit. In this way, a cost becomes a profit in a way that is mutually beneficial to the firm, the environment, and the surrounding community—a "win-win-win." This basic example helps to explain the notions of sustainable and mutual profits, showing how they are related and how both concepts might be practically implemented as a new management technique. While this specific example is about natural capital, similar approaches can be applicable to human and social capital to derive sustainable and mutual levels of profits that account for the costs and benefits of maintaining these other forms of capital.

In conclusion, while there is nothing yet big enough to replace existing capital, we must now work to develop it. We do not underestimate the task. In 1995, Professor C. K. Prahalad asked, "Why can't we create inclusive capitalism?" Eleven years later, he published a book titled The Fortune at the Bottom of the Pyramid, outlining why he thought inclusive capitalism could work by drawing the majority of the world's poor into profitably productive work. He argued that the billions of souls at the so-called "base of the pyramid" financially—the poorest of the poor—is where the greatest opportunities can be found for entrepreneurship.

After another decade has passed, however, that goal still remains an elusive one, though we believe Prahalad was essentially correct. What was missing from his original conception, in our view, was the measurement of different types of correlative capital and the idea of like-for-like remuneration of the various capitals. The promising results of our work thus far in bringing entrepreneurial opportunities to the poor in Nairobi, Manila, and very soon in Uganda and Côte d'Ivoire (then China, India, and elsewhere) will make this assertion even more compelling as additional supporting evidence from different markets is gathered.

Conclusion

Repositioning Business as a Restorative Healing Power

We're never in lack of money. We lack people with
dreams, [people] who can die for those dreams.

Jack Ma, Founder and Executive Chairman,
Alibaba Group

Every few decades, it is time to rewrite the rules about what generates value for a business. We believe we are now at another such historical juncture, where systemic change is on our doorstep and the rewriting of the rules for business must urgently begin.

There are many signs indicating the global economic system has reached the end of a cycle—an end to the era where trust in money alone was paramount, and the accumulation of financial capital was the ultimate objective. We are witnessing, for example, a shift in the economic center of gravity from the West to the East, with the traditional G7 industrialized economies (the United States, Germany, Britain, Japan, France, Italy, and Canada) now representing just 10 percent of the world's population, while China has become the world's foremost creditor and Africa, with its fast-growing population and relatively low-density land mass, bringing an abundance of human and natural resources.

The "old" industrialized countries may still account for about 40 percent of the global economy, but their influence is shrinking at an accelerated pace. While the West is waning, the rest of the world is busily giving rise to a new middle class ascending from the so-called base of the (economic) pyramid, adding the rough equivalent of a new "Germany" in terms of economic size every three to five years. This astounding growth of the middle class outside the traditional West will bring additional stresses on natural resources and will require the global economy to create hundreds of millions of new jobs to meet the spiking demand for employment. Together, such realities constitute a unique opportunity to create a new culture of prosperity for the many, reversing the trend among the most mature economies of widening wealth disparity that, in turn, has been a contributing factor to growing societal stress and even to some of the violence and populism we are witnessing across the Western world.

The shift from financial capital scarcity in the 1970s to other forms of scarcity today (social, human, and natural capital) is well described in this book. Similarly, and perhaps of greater importance, we have discussed the reality of the shift we are seeing today from an industrial and service economy, where the ownership of industrial and financial assets were of greatest value, to a knowledge and digital economy, where the ownership of relationships, social networks, access to data, and so on are central. Klaus Schwab, executive chairman of the World Economic Forum, describes this shift and its extension as a "Fourth Industrial Revolution" in his book of the same name.[1] Schwab's conviction that the exponential technological advances we are witnessing that are fusing the physical, digital, and biological worlds—such as "ubiquitous mobile supercomputing, intelligent robots, self-driving cars, neuro-technological brain enhancements, and genetic editing"—are, in his words, "fundamentally changing the way we live, work, and relate to one another." We could not agree more, but would add that it is the combination of the technologies and the reality of the new scarcities that have brought us to the brink of economic collapse and reinvention, since the old economic model through which business has operated for nearly half a century is no longer capable of functioning optimally within the new context and, in fact, is doomed to a greater spiraling dysfunction that simply is not sustainable.

A number of increasingly visible cracks in the system are becoming obvious to those looking for them. The destructive, almost irrational market overfocus on short-term maximization of earnings extracted for shareholders rather than reinvested in the value chains of stakeholders is one such example of dysfunction. The transformation of the role of money from being an instrument to provide liquidity into a high-intensity instrument of speculation and wealth accumulation is another example, and has led to the structural misallocation of resources driven by this short-term thinking. The degradation of the self-regulating mechanism of the financial markets should be of great concern, as should be the increase in size and frequency of financial crises playing out as it has over the last four decades, with the high (or low, depending upon perspective) water mark coming in late 2008. The next shock to the system could, in fact, be the one that will precipitate the collapse of the last hollow remnants of the current system and its replacement by a new system.

History teaches us that this kind of transition from one form of economic system to another is never easy or painless. The subprime crisis of 2008 continues to inflict pain, especially on the many millions who are as a result either unemployed or underemployed, not to mention the growing despair and shattered dreams among the next generation that they will ever find career paths that will at least equal if not surpass the livelihoods of their parents and grandparents. "The only surprise about the economic crisis of 2008 was that it came as a surprise to so many," said Nobel laureate Joseph Stiglitz in his book Freefall. He continued: "For a few observers, it was a textbook case that was not only predictable but also predicted." The International Monetary Fund's October 2016 announcement that global (private and public) debt has reached a staggering record of $152 trillion—more than double the size of the entire global economy— highlights the fact that the next crisis, which may be far more disruptive than the crisis that began in 2008, is also predictable, and we predict it will come sooner than many may think.

The pain of transition

The main response to the continuing crisis from the fully industrialized old economies, which may very well segue into the next, bigger (decisive) one, has been to grow the money supply at staggering rates through quantitative easing (QE) strategies. The QE was named innocuously perhaps to make more palatable the "printing" of huge sums of money essentially from nothing—with no true underlying value except the confidence of the people that there is a value to what John Tamny of Forbes magazine described in his 2014 article "The Fed Is Not Printing Money, It's Doing Something Much Worse" as "the corruption of money's sole purpose as a stable medium of exchange."

There has, as yet, been no meaningful effort to effect systemic change before systemic change is by natural circumstances forced upon us abruptly and painfully. Instead, doing more of the same seems to dominantly characterize the lack of imagination of the central bankers and government leaders in the face of imminent change. Such loose monetary policies, carried on to this degree, are nurturing the financial assets bubble, thereby creating the conditions for a future crisis that may well dwarf the last one. There is now a dysfunctional gap between financial assets inflation and real consumer goods inflation. This has even spurred negative interest rates in some situations that many are now beginning to call the "new normal" rather than the very rare exception.

Negative interest rates send a dangerous implicit signal across the markets that there is no longer an incentive to invest in the future; that there is no hope in the current economy to create growth and prosperity in the future. QEs are also a sign of surrender in that governments now feel they have no choice but to artificially invest with what is essentially faux currency— something allegedly of value that is created from nothing. Negative rates, moreover, confirm that the value of financial capital is decreasing, even withering, which is a situation that can be sustained for only a temporary period of time, but will gradually undermine the whole foundation of the system if it is prolonged.

We are now forced to rethink a new global financial order and the role of financial capital in the new economic context. As investors, the options we have today are essentially either to invest in government bonds or other financial assets with near zero or negative interest rates, which means losing, or we can invest at a risk in the real economy and specifically in businesses that know how to manage the other forms of capital described in this book. But investing in the new economy is truly a new frontier, with the nature of risk shifting from what in the old economy was purely a financial risk management exercise (via a cohort of complex financial engineering products) to something entirely different.

Mitigating the risks in managing a basket of multiple new forms of capital, not surprisingly, will be more complex than mitigating risks from a single form of capital. Not all business practices to mobilize and deploy social, human, and natural capital to benefit a wider range of stakeholders will work in every business situation or in every business culture. Hence, a new breed of entrepreneurial managers must be willing and allowed to experiment with a mix of different management practices around the different forms of capital—and be rewarded for risk taking, not penalized for every failure, as with true entrepreneurs. There really is no choice in the matter. Either we adapt, and quickly, or we perish. As Stiglitz notes in Freefall, "If no action is taken to manage the global financial and global economic system better, there will be more, and possibly worse, crises in the future."

Fresh thinking born of very old truths

The new rules of the new economy actually are not really so new, in truth. In fact, they come from an ancient concept about the role and priorities of the key pillars of prosperity in any economic system—people, planet, and profit. They are rooted in the deep recesses of our culture, history, and human identity. This is called the principle of the Jubilee, whereby caring sufficiently for each form of capital and seeking mutually beneficial rather than exploitative relationships constitute the norm rather than the exception. Embedded within the Jubilee way is recognition of the need for some financial capital accumulation, in the hands of talented entrepreneurs, to grow prosperity, so this is not about equalizing asset allocation through redistribution, but rather about giving the responsibility for managing the financial capital to those gifted to do this. The same is true for managing the other forms of capital, as long as the intent is to grow prosperity holistically to benefit the many rather than the few or just the individual at the expense of the others.

The Jubilee is also about resetting the norms every so often to ensure that everyone, at given waypoints in their journey through life, has a chance to begin again without the burden of debt. In this way, the risk of excessive capital accumulation over an excessive period of time, during which the many would be left in an overly disadvantaged circumstance, is mitigated. Misusing financial capital for highly risky speculation and solely for wealth accumulation purposes is also rendered less possible through this approach.

What is new, perhaps, is that these principles can now be enacted as natural laws for doing business, and not just as inspiring but seemingly impractical philosophical principles. There is a better way of doing business, and one through which more are rewarded for their participation, on multiple levels. This means that doing good for society and for the planet can actually come about through business practices without coming always at the expense of financial capital. "Win-win-win" scenarios across the value chains of business actually are possible and can bring about superior, holistic value creation that will make businesses more sustainable in terms of their continued success in the marketplace over time. And in this way, businesses can bring about societal and environmental transformation in ways that governments and charities cannot.

An environment conducive for a systemic shift

The emergence of negative interest rates and the prospect of this becoming the "new normal" has opened a window of opportunity to rethink what the role of money should be in the new economic context. Negative rates leave investors with no real choice but to redirect financial flows away from financial markets—the bond markets with their near zero to below zero returns and the stock markets which are presently very overvalued—to other forms of investment that are not focused on short-term financial gains. Such investments in the real economy, like housing, infrastructure, and education, especially among impoverished communities, can have higher returns than zero or negative rates are providing, as we have seen through our piloting business experiments to date.

As a reminder, the approach underpinning those pilots—with its modest number of key variables and a shared value index that can be used across the different forms of capital—can be briefly summarized as follows:

Key Features	**Parsimonious:** Each capital can be measured through a small number of variables accounting for approximately 75%+ of each of the different forms of capital.
	Stable and actionable: Each capital and their corresponding metrics have been tested across several countries and several business situations, on both the demand and supply sides, and they exhibit remarkable stability.
	Related to performance: A strong and stable correlation between these new forms of capital with economic performance has been established in a number of business situations.
Human Capital	An individual's skills, experience, knowledge, satisfaction (general and job specific), health, and well-being.
	Measured through an adapted "well-being at work" survey measuring the following:
	❖ **Corporate identity.** "Walk the talk"—to what extent employees align with the firm's values, identity, corporate vision, and business strategy.
	❖ **Employee social capital.** Perceived level of trust relationships among employees and between employees and management.
	❖ **POUM (prospect of upward mobility) effect.** The extent to which employees accept a greater differentiation of wages inside their firm as long as they hope to progress upward in wage distribution.

Human Capital (*continued*)	❖ **Status and recognition.** The symbolic value of the job in terms of the power and prestige it confers to the employee. A partial substitute for wage disparity. ❖ **Line manager effect.** The extent to which a positively engaged and satisfied line manager impacts the level of well-being at work of his/her direct report. In impoverished communities, the following factors were identified: ❖ **General well-being.** Level of satisfaction with respect to income, health care, housing, and wealth, the extent to which expenditure demands are met. ❖ **Job-specific well-being.** Working conditions (time, workload, flexibility, job demands, material and equipment), social capital (support from the communities of suppliers, customers, other participant in the program).
Social Capital	Nonfinancial relationships that affect a person's well-being and prosperity. Measured by survey through three key drivers: trust, community cohesion, and capacity for collective action. ❖ **Social cohesion.** The extent that differences in identity (gender, religion, ethnicity, etc.) and status (land ownership, education, class, etc.) are perceived as sources of division or distance among people in their wider community and in their business network. ❖ **Trust and behavior.** The perceived degree of trust in key social and business action (lending/borrowing money, or expectations for moral and responsible behavior to be displayed). ❖ **Capacity for collective action:** How the members of a community solve their problems through working together (mobilizing resources for collective purposes, petitioning authorities, working collaboratively toward common objectives, etc).

continues ▶

Natural Capital	The complete input flow of natural resources used across the entire value chain of a product.
	Designed to impact performance through resources (natural capital) efficiency.
	Measured through five main metrics:
	❖ **Nonrenewable abiotic materials.** Nonrenewable resources (e.g., metals, minerals)
	❖ **Renewable biotic materials.** Renewable resources (e.g., organic materials, vegetation, living organisms)
	❖ **Water.** Rainfall, spring sources, domestic
	❖ **Air.** Oxygen absorbed through combustion
	❖ **Topsoil erosion.** From deforestation, soil salinization (impact on biodiversity)
Shared Financial Capital	How the economic benefits are shared among a value chain's participants, in order to ensure a sustainable margin and wage.
	Designed to impact performance through more equitable (shared financial capital) distribution of benefits to stakeholders in a value chain.
	Measurable through a "shared value" index throughout the value chain (similar to a Gini index):
	❖ To assess value sharing and identify hot spots to address
	❖ To develop comparisons (across value chain, over time)
	❖ To provide a good framework for assessment

Regardless of the simplicity and actionability of the approach, a movement will be required for the kind of paradigm shift in thinking to take place about the value of capitals beyond the financial. Thankfully, we are seeing signs of just such a movement beginning to emerge. This phenomenon is not driven by activists or ideologists, but rather is being nurtured— consciously or subconsciously—by a small but influential number of long-thinking business leaders who could, using the prior analogy of the collapse of the Soviet Union, be the proverbial Gorbachevs of our time, but for business. These leaders, who number among them true captains of industry, know the ways of business from the inside, are challenging traditional thinking more openly, intuitively understand the fundamental flaws of the current approach, and perhaps most importantly are trying hard to find a new way before the system collapses upon itself and leaves their firms in a disadvantaged position.

One can "see" the rumblings of such thinking in the artifacts many consider to be central strongholds of the financial capitalism system. Larry Fink, for example, the chief executive of Black-Rock—the world's largest investor, managing $4.5 trillion—said in a February 2016 public letter to senior executives of S&P 500 companies and large European corporations that "today's culture of quarterly earnings hysteria is totally contrary to the long-term approach we need." He went on to explain that "generating sustainable returns over time requires a sharper focus not only on governance, but also on environmental and social factors facing companies today. These issues offer both risks and opportunities, but for too long companies have not considered them core to their business—even when the world's political leaders are increasingly focused on them, as demonstrated by the Paris Climate Accord. Over the long-term, environmental, social and governance (ESG) issues—ranging from climate change to diversity to board effectiveness—have real and quantifiable financial impacts."

Paul Poleman, chief executive of Unilever, one of the world's leading fast-moving consumer goods (FMCG) companies, has been equally blunt in public interviews about his firm's ten-point Sustainable Living Plan: "I don't think our fiduciary duty is to put shareholders first," said Poleman. "I say the opposite. What we firmly believe is that if we focus our company on improving the lives of the world's citizens and come up with genuine sustainable solutions, we are more in sync with consumers and society and ultimately this will result in good shareholder returns." Poleman has also observed publicly that "the very essence of capitalism is under threat as business is now seen as a personal wealth accumulator. We have to bring this world back to sanity and put the greater good ahead of self-interest. We need to fight very hard to create an environment out there that is more long-term focused and move away from short-termism."

One of Asia's most successful entrepreneurs, Jack Ma, whose Alibaba Group is widely described as the "Amazon.com of China," is publicly quoted as believing that "today, making money is very simple. But making sustainable money while being responsible to the society and improving the world is very difficult." Ma goes on to explain: "If you want to grow, find a good opportunity today. If you want to be a great company, think about what social problem you could solve."

Such unorthodox thinking among titans of business like Fink, Poleman, and Ma, among others, are amplified by such aspirational global initiatives as the UN Millennium Development Goals, which aimed by 2015 to "eradicate extreme poverty and hunger; achieve universal primary education; promote gender equality and empower women; reduce child mortality; improve maternal health; combat HIV/AIDS, malaria, and other diseases; ensure environmental sustainabilty; and develop global partnerships on development." Failing to achieve these lofty aspirations, the goals were updated/replaced in 2015 by the UN Sustainable Development Goals (to be reached by 2030), which seek to end poverty and hunger; promote health, gender equality, clean water and sanitation, affordable clean energy, decent work, and economic growth; to build industry, innovation, and infrastructure; reduce inequalities; make cities and communities more sustainable; drive responsible consumption;

take action on climate change; improve life below water and on the land; promote peace and justice; and forge partnerships to achieve these goals.

While such ambitions are laudable, the contrast between what international institutions and governments aspire to achieve and what the Larry Finks, Paul Polemans, Jack Mas, and others in the realm of business can practically deliver—if equipped with a new model with new metrics and management practices to drive superior holistic performance—is a stark one. Business, in our view, is much more likely to move the world from the aspirational to the practical in terms of transformational lasting change, provided business leaders are convinced that a new way is available to them to "do good, and do well, at scale." Business won't be transformational, however, if it only has the tools to make trade-offs between doing good and doing well, which limits the prospect of adequate scaling up.

The roles and responsibilities of business in the new economic context, especially of MNCs, are evolving and growing in importance, making it difficult to imagine how so many business leaders can still be clinging to what now seems an archaic Friedmanic concept of "the sole social responsibility of business is to maximize profit for distribution to shareholders." Today, MNCs—along with a small number of very large nonprofit organizations—are de facto the only truly "complete" actors of globalization in that only they can operate almost freely across the world with few exceptions, such as in a completely closed economy like North Korea. MNCs also have the means to address global challenges in ways that nation-states cannot, hence, they may be the only actors that can (re)shape the new world in which we are living. This reality brings upon MNC leaders an enormous responsibility for which most are not yet practically or emotionally equipped to address. The true responsibility of the firm today extends far beyond its traditional legal boundaries and must embrace the whole value chain or business ecosystem in which companies operate. But the existing legal framework does not yet support this extended responsibility, creating a new role for policymakers to adjust the corporate law corpus.

Evaluating the true performance of the firm must also evolve far beyond that of financial capital alone and will require business leaders to flex new muscles that are still mostly unknown to them. Friedman has given us the ability to manage financial capital in very robust ways, and those who have embraced his philosophies to the extreme have gone on to demonstrate how money can be made from money through clever financial engineering, derivatives trading, and other methods, and even how money can be made from nothing through central bank-executed unconventional monetary policies like quantitative easing. Managing value beyond the purely financial, however, is a new discipline, but one that is beginning to take root and grow, as we have discussed. This multi-capital approach requires more than willingness and an open mind. It requires a whole new range of business practices, not all of which will work in every corporation's cultural context, so time is needed, and a movement of like-purposed partnering companies can significantly accelerate the production of actionable insights.

Along with new management practices must come new metrics for human, social, and natural capital that can proactively drive performance rather than just passively measure impact of activities, although our metrics are multipurpose and can do both. Impact metrics (lagging indicators), however, are less central to our model, whereas management metrics (leading indicators) are what we want to better understand and deploy, as they give managers a means to mobilize, access, and leverage "riches" inherent in people and the environment that have hitherto been hidden or largely ignored by business, mainly because they were not considered to be measurable in a business-actionable fashion. Hence, we believe the contribution of our work to provide management with generic, stable, actionable (at a business unit level), non-monetized metrics for human, social, and natural capital is the kind of breakthrough that has transformational potential for the way business is conducted.

The main contribution of this business model initiative could indeed serve multiple purposes. First, it is highlighting the shortcomings of the current financial capitalism model and the lack of a suitable academic (management theory) and business (practices) framework to address the new rules of the game of the emerging global economic system. Next, we are showing through business piloting activities how it is possible right now to begin to address these systemic shortcomings. We are making the case that large businesses, especially MNCs, now have the power, influence, and responsibility to act more responsibly on behalf of the stakeholders in their value chains—and that they must step up to this challenge—though many are not yet culturally, emotionally, or intellectually equipped to accept all of this needed change. And we are challenging what it means for a business to be responsible; that traditional legal boundaries of the firm are no longer sufficient parameters to determine how far business should reach because increasingly complex business value chains are only as strong as the weakest link in those chains.

The true purpose of what might be considered a great company in the future is not just to make more money for shareholders alone. It is more about how they can thoughtfully and intentionally consider what social problem(s) they can solve by leveraging the power of their enterprise for this purpose. This is a challenge to the narrow perspective that business performance is about financial performance alone, so the great companies will need to expand their balance sheets to include how they (positively and negatively) impact social, human, and natural capital across their business ecosystems of stakeholders, now that it is possible to measure these other capitals with the same degree of accuracy, simplicity, and actionability as financial capital is measured. Such firms will be those who grasp that business can simultaneously drive both profits and wider mutual benefits for people and planet by understanding and managing these multiple forms of capital.

The responsibility of knowledge

The journey from ignorance to enlightenment is not unlike the journey from astrology to astronomy. The journey from profit maximization for shareholders to making business more mutual for stakeholders is not dissimilar to this analogy. This journey has begun, but it is still at an early stage, with many corporate initiatives more closely resembling astrology rather than astronomy in that there is much more aspiration than science behind them. Moreover, few such initiatives have the kind of robust metrics behind them that can drive greater holistic business performance. This may explain why the emphasis today remains weighted toward CSR and sustainability programs—doing good for people and planet at a cost, while aiming to boost corporate reputation—rather than trying for the kind of systemic transformation that will come about when business realizes it can solve social and environmental challenges at a profit.

Every stage on this journey from ignorance to enlightenment is important, as each brings additional knowledge and the responsibility to act that comes with it. In the words of Franklin Roosevelt, "Great power involves great responsibility," and the rising awareness of the new role and responsibility of business in society now emerging from some stakeholders (select business leaders, government regulators, academics, and consumers) is a reassuring sign of the capacity of humanity to adapt and adjust to new realities, in this instance, to the new global economic context. Similarly, the recent Sustainability Development Goals of the UN are encouraging. Yet, as Albert Einstein said, "no problem can be solved from the same level of consciousness that created it," just as no one should "pour new wine into old wineskins," according to the old adage, as "both the wine and wineskins will be ruined." The adage continues: "Instead, new wine should be poured into new wineskins."

Initiatives like the Millennium Development Goals or Sustainability Development Goals, placed as they are within proverbial "old wineskins," might bear little fruit at the end of the day. Hence, we are aiming to address the issue at its root to trigger the kind of systemic reformation that will reinstate the role of money in business to what it should be—a means of economic exchange and of distributing ownership rather than of a pseudo-commodity meant to be infinitely accumulated. Money can and should still be a powerful instrument, but one that is so because it is in service of the economy rather than the most valued output of the economy.

An equally important part of our objective is the proper remuneration of each different form of capital and the reinstatement of nonfinancial capitals valuing the contribution of human beings, societies, and nature to a position of economic preeminence. The (re)discovery of the central role that human, social, and natural capital can play—if properly managed—in driving economic performance is the key to achieving this realignment of priorities. When the realignment begins to scale up, financial capital and the financial system itself should revert to the role of "good servant," as we have seen the damage money can do as a "bad master." Money needs to be remunerated like a good servant rather than a master, hence, the concept of there being a "right" level of profit for the firm—the basis of the extraordinary question posed to us almost two years before the 2008 crisis that launched this remarkable journey.

One of the most important tools of management is the measurement of profit. Determining what is the "right" profit for the company has from the outset been the overarching objective of our new business model program. Existing measures of profit, as we have explained in this book, are not complete—and are actually misleading—in so far as they do not correctly account for the maintenance of the firm's capital. Conventional measures of profit are defined as the net of the cost of maintaining physical capital—plant, machinery, buildings, inventories, etc.—but do not take into account the cost of maintaining other forms of capital, such as human, social, and natural capital. Such measures, therefore, substantially overstate the true profit of the firm because they fail to reflect the actual cost of doing business in maintaining the nonfinancial forms of capital.

As we have argued herein, it is possible that the right level of profit for a firm might actually be higher than existing accounting measures tell us. For example, it is possible to develop commercially viable solutions (i.e., financially profitable) to either address issues created by a commercial activity or to leverage hidden riches that were not hitherto harness-able. To address a commercial activity that has a negative impact on natural capital, like water pollution, it may be possible to offset the cost of restoring the capital (the cost of the technology needed to clean the water after it is contaminated through business use), but to do it in such a way that the technology has a dual function, such as more efficiently extracting ethanol from corn, as one plausible example. This could potentially convert an investment cost into a profit, thereby providing both an environmental good and a good-for-business outcome. In the Maua micro-distribution/ micro-entrepreneurship initiative in Kenya, where we have identified human and social capital in places where there is no (or very little) visible financial capital, we are intentionally managing and growing these nonfinancial capitals to deliver social good, human well-being, and stable incomes (at higher margins than usual), while generating as an outcome higher growth and profit for the MNC. In a way, this approach is a means to convert what were the hidden riches of the impoverished or of the environment, measured in social, human, or natural capital assets, into profit for all involved.

Historically, the type of dysfunction we observe today—visible in such conditions as the stress on natural resources, environmental degradation, widening wealth disparity, and even the fact that many rights groups now say there are more slaves today than at any point in human history—is often resolved through one or a mix of the following:

❖ Natural or social disasters, such as famine, wars, revolutions, or epidemics.

❖ The conquest of new land, such as "Manifest Destiny" or what could soon be space colonization.

❖ Scientific or technological breakthroughs; a new economic model that manages new forms of scarcity, allocates resources, and redistributes value creation differently.

The solutions coming from new science and technology, and from new business models, are far preferable than the other historical solutions, which can inflict great suffering on the world. But to paraphrase Winston Churchill, "You can often count on human beings to do the right thing—after they have tried everything else."

We now have what may be a once-in-a-generation opportunity to reposition business as a restorative, healing power for the global economy. Business can and must become an engine for profound positive change for the many, and management science can become a discipline that can create and harvest the true riches of the new century. In the wise words of King Solomon in the book of Ecclesiastes, "There is a time for everything, a time to keep and a time to throw away; a time to plant and a time to uproot; a time to speak and a time to stay silent." We believe it is the time to uproot and discard the dysfunctions of financial capitalism; to sow the seeds of a more complete form of capitalism; to speak about what we are learning through education and business; to share that there is a way to heal business and that the healing of business can bring about greater healing in the world—of relationships among mankind and between mankind and nature. We invite you to join in this journey of discovery with us.

Afterword

by Lim Siong Guan

Completing Capitalism: Heal Business to Heal the World is a thoughtful look at where all good business and social initiatives need to get to. So it is essential reading and essential thinking for all leaders who want to be "in time for the future."

Some readers may consider the ideas to be ahead of their time. But they will be wrong. Not thinking through the ideas will be falling behind in time.

Everything we do needs to have a worthy purpose. Completing Capitalism makes us think about the purpose of capitalism. Should it be only about lifting the wealth of shareholders, or should it be also about boosting the well-being of everyone who has a stake in the life and purpose of the enterprise?

Economics is the rational allocation of scarce resources. And financial metrics have been the standard way by which to measure the sensibleness of the decisions. However, financial capital is not what is lacking in the world today. So why should financial metrics be the only perspective for good decisions in the allocation and utilization of resources for meeting the needs of people wherever they may be in the world?

What is very much lacking today is good deployment and utilization of human capital for improved productivity and an engaged workforce, good generation of social capital for well-functioning communities, and good exploitation of natural capital for the well-being of future generations.

Human capital relates to people. How can people be encouraged and developed to be the best they can be? How does each person attain the best chances to realize their potential in intellect, knowledge, skills, and experience? How well is everyone motivated and enabled to do their best and contribute the most they can? And how are all their efforts synergized so that the business or organization is the best it can be? On the principle that "what gets measured gets done," we need good measures on the deployment and utilization of human capital. This book offers interesting, practical ideas.

Many organizations call for teamwork and collaboration as essential virtues for sound operations and congenial workplaces. Social capital is the grease that makes people look out for each other and makes human beings "human." People yearn for identity; they seek to be loved, they seek to be respected. We need to measure our accretion or depletion of social capital for the sake of "knowing what is going on" among our workers and communities. This book offers insightful, enlightening perspectives.

The world speaks much about climate change and the overuse of natural resources. We need to be good stewards of our world. This is no soft-headed notion. It is enlightened self-interest for the generations to come. Whether it be air and water, oil and gas, or sand and minerals, we need a way to measure how we utilize the natural capital at our disposal. This book offers sound, thoughtful viewpoints.

Financial measurement offers just a singular, narrow perspective on whether a business is being run in a sustainable, effective manner. A comprehensive slate of measures that goes beyond looking at financial capital but also covers human capital, social capital, and natural capital is urgently needed to give us a complete picture of the sustainability of success in what we are doing.

Completing Capitalism offers a practical, holistic perspective on the responsible, sustainable leadership of business. If leadership is "making good things happen which on their own would not happen," every leader must give due attention to the urgency in the call to do what is good and right in delivering on our responsibility for sustained success into the future. To "wait and see" is to "wait and die."

All of us want to succeed in work and life. This book makes the point that if we do not measure what we are doing in a comprehensive way, we may well be on the wrong track. Indeed, our instincts tell us that we cannot be on the right track if our workers feel disengaged in their jobs, new employees are merely "satisficing" in their job delivery, the clarion call for "work-life balance" suggests that work is not fun but a "necessary evil" for earning what is necessary to "enjoy life," members of societies show little concern for their fellow citizens, "me-centeredness" seems to have totally crowded out "other-centeredness," decisions are made for the comforts of today's generation with little thought for the next two generations . . . the list goes on!

Completing Capitalism seeks to offer maximum freedom for business to realize optimal, sustainable, long-term success for the business, its people and the communities they operate in, and our planet. And it does so by offering useful ways by which to measure what we are doing and to address the gaps in our actions. They are actionable metrics for transformational effect. The future is now! We must not miss the turn.

—Professor Lim Siong Guan, *Lee Kuan Yew School of Public Policy, National University of Singapore; former group President (2007–2016) of GIC, fund manager for Singapore's foreign financial reserves; Chairman of Honour (Singapore), a charity promoting the virtue of honor for the well-being of the nation; coauthor of* The Leader, The Teacher, & You *(Imperial College Press, 2014) and* Winning with Honour *(Imperial College Press, 2016).*

Notes

Foreword

1. See the three articles published in Brewery Journal #3 (January 2014) dedicated to "Exploring Mutuality": the editorial by Stephen M. Badger II, Guest Editor and Chairman of the Board, Mars, Incorporated; "The Mars Mutuality Journey" by Paul S. Michaels, President, Mars, Incorporated; and "The Economics of Mutuality" by Bruno B. Roche and Jay F. Jakub, Catalyst, Mars, Incorporated. Source: www.freuds.com/the-brewery.

Introduction

1. Again, a point of reference for understanding the roots of the economics of mutuality is the special edition of the Brewery Journal (no. 3, January 2014) dedicated to "Exploring Mutuality." Source: www.freuds.com/the-brewery.
2. Still ongoing with Oxford University's Saïd Business School as part of the collaborative research platform called Mutuality in Business: Adoption and Impact of Mutuality Metrics. Source: www.sbs.ox.ac.uk /faculty-research/research-projects/mutuality-business.
3. Global Footprint Network is an independent think tank that is known for computing the Ecological Debt Day (also known as Earth Overshoot Day), which is the day when humanity has exhausted nature's budget for the year.
4. Jubilee is an ancient concept that refers to a fifty-year cycle whereby slaves are emancipated, land is returned to its former owners, and cultivation of the land is temporarily suspended to allow for rest and regeneration.

Chapter 1

1. The labor share is the part of national income allocated to labor compensation, while the capital share is the part of national income going to capital. A falling labor share often reflects more rapid growth in labor productivity than in average labor compensation, and an increase in returns to capital relative to labor.
2. The Labour Share in G20 Economies. Report prepared for the G20 Employment Working Group, Antalya, Turkey, February 26–27, 2015.
3. Source: Global Footprint Network 2016, http://www.footprintnetwork.org.
4. A derivative is a traded security whose price is derived from one or more underlying assets. The derivatives market is estimated by some

analysts to be more than ten times the size of the total gross domestic product of the entire global economy and may actually be as much as the unimaginable sum of $1.2 quadrillion. Although there is not a consensus about the actual size of the derivatives market—as it may vary dramatically whether the focus is on the market value or the notional value—it is still staggering, and whatever the calculation methods, derivatives comprise an impressive proportion of worldwide investments.

5. Brian Merchant, "How Many Gallons of Water Does It Take to Make . . ." Treehugger.com, June 24, 2009.

6. United Nations University—Institute for Water, Environment, and Health.

Chapter 2

1. Peter Warr, "Well-Being and the Workplace," in Well-Being: The Foundations of Hedonic Psychology, eds. Daniel Kahneman, Edward Diener, and Norbert Schwartz (New York: Russell Sage Foundation, 1999), 392–412.

2. J. K. Harter, F. L. Schmidt, J. W. Asplund, E. A. Killham, and S. Agrawal, "Causal Impact of Employee Work Perceptions on the Bottom Line of Organizations," Perspectives on Psychological Science 5, (2010): 378–389.

3. A. Edmans, "Does the Stock Market Fully Value Intangibles? Employee Satisfaction and Equity Prices," Journal of Financial Economics 101 (2011): 621–640.

4. P. Böckerman and P. Ilmakunnas, "The Job Satisfaction-Productivity Nexus: A Study Using Matched Survey and Register Data," Industrial and Labor Relations Review 65 (2012): 244–262.

5. M. Riketta, "The Causal Relation Between Job Attitudes and Performance: A Meta-Analysis of Panel Studies," Journal of Applied Psychology 93 (2008): 472–481.

Chapter 3

1. A point of reference for understanding the concept of social capital as studied by economists is the chapter written by Steven Durlauf and Marcel Fafchamps in Handbook of Economic Growth, vol. 1 (2005), chapter 26.

2. Marcel Mauss, "Essai sur le don. Forme et raison de l'échange dans les sociétés archaïques," L'année sociologique Tome 1 (1990): 30–186 (The Gift: The Form and Reason for Exchange in Archaic Societies).

3. Pierre Bourdieu, "The Forms of Capital" in Handbook of Theory and Research for the Sociology of Education, ed. John C. Richardson (New York: Greenwood Press, 1986), 241–258.

4. Francis Fukuyama, "Social Capital and Civil Society" (IMF Working Paper 74, 2000).

5. C. Grootaert, D. Narayan, V. Nyhan Jones, and M. Woolcock, "Measuring Social Capital: An Integrated Questionnaire" (World Bank Working Paper no. 18, 2004).

Chapter 4

1. Natural capital, as we define it for our purposes in a business context, is simply the value of raw materials used in the manufacture of goods.
2. In this model, inputs refer to all resources that are used for a specific activity, and outputs are all direct effects of the activity. Outcomes are the short- to mid-term effects caused by the outputs, while impacts are defined as long-term effects of the outcomes. Source: Justus von Geibler, Francesco Cordaro, Katharina Kennedy, Michael Lettenmeier, and Bruno Roche, "Integrating Resource Efficiency in Business Strategies: A Mixed-Method Approach for Environmental Life Cycle Assessment In the Single-Serve Coffee Value Chain," Journal of Cleaner Production 115 (2016): 62–74.
3. Justus von Geibler et al, "Integrating Resource Efficiency in Business Strategies," 62–74.
4. Factor Four is a concept introduced by Ernst von Weizsacker and the Wuppertal Institute, along with Hunter and Amory Lovins of the Rocky Mountain Institute, suggesting that with existing technologies, business can reduce by 75 percent the natural resources it consumes through a focus on inputs efficiency, while raising productivity fourfold. Its more ambitious successor concept, called Factor Ten, takes the Factor Four theory further, suggesting mankind must reduce inputs by 90 percent over the next thirty to fifty years, while raising resource productivity tenfold, given the rate of resource depletion.

Chapter 5

1. PPP approximates the adjustments needed to calculate the relative value of a currency to a local currency.

Chapter 6

1. Rich in terms of social and human capital but poor in terms of financial capital (with a majority below the poverty line).
2. A point of reference for understanding the hybrid value chain concept is the Harvard Business Review article "A New Alliance for Global Change" by Bill Drayton and Valeria Budinich, from the September 2010 issue.
3. Technoserve is a Washington, DC, based international nonprofit organization that develops business solutions to address poverty issues in developing countries. Source: www.technoserve.org.

Conclusion

1. Klaus Schwab, The Fourth Industrial Revolution (New York: Crown Business, 2017).

Acknowledgments

We would like to express our deep appreciation and gratitude to the many people whose work contributed to key pieces of the story behind this book, and to the business leaders and family shareholders of Mars, Incorporated, for allowing us to publish this book and to pursue what has become a vocational endeavor for us. We would like to especially thank our colleague, Dr. Francesco Cordaro, for his groundbreaking research, partnering with Professor Alain Desdoigts from the Sorbonne and Professor Marcel Fafchamps from Stanford, on social capital measurement; Professor Claudia Senik from the Paris School of Economics on human capital measurement; and Dr. Justus von Geibler and his team at the Wuppertal Institute in Germany on natural capital measurement. Similarly, we would like to recognize the tireless efforts of our dear colleague in Singapore, Clara Shen, who with a small, dedicated team brilliantly led the hybrid value chain piloting of experimental businesses based on the new model and metrics across complex environments like Nairobi, Manila, now Jakarta, and soon China and beyond.

We would also like to thank our inspiring friend, noted author Peter Block, for his sage advice and for recommending our manuscript to our new friend and now publisher, Steve Piersanti. Thanks to the incomparable Professor Avishay Braverman, who wisely advises and assists us in opening new doors, including to his wonderful Bedouin Israeli friends in the Negev outside the Beersheba of Genesis, where we hope to take the new model one day to help reconcile the sons of Ishmael and of Isaac. We have been immensely blessed by the wisdom, friendship, and support of Dr. Frank Akers, our "man from Gad" who co-chairs the Mars Science Advisory Council. He is a former director of Oak Ridge National Laboratory and chaired both external peer reviews of our work that endorsed it, paving the way for the beginning of the model's adoption by parts of the business and its teaching at Oxford University and soon elsewhere. Thanks to Professor Peter Berger, our "resident sociologist," who helped us crack the social capital measurement challenge with help from our partnering anthropologists, especially Dr. Paige West of Columbia University and Dr. Amy Stambach of Wisconsin University and Oxford University; to Dr. Steve Garber, a very dear friend and quiet advisor who has shared this journey with us from the outset, introducing us to many fascinating contributors along the way; and to Michael Ramsden, Tomas Sandell, Arleen Westerhof, Andrew Baker, George Annadorai, Patrick McDonald and his team, and all the other friends who encouraged us along the way.

There are many more deserving recognition—too many to list—but a special thanks goes to former Mars CEO and friend, Paul Michaels, who initially championed our model when it was merely a crazy-sounding idea, and to Olivier Goudet, CEO of what has become the largest coffee sourcing company in the world, JAB Holdings, for his encouragement and support dating back to his service as Mars' chief financial officer. It was at Olivier's urging, in fact, that we undertook writing this book. Thanks to Martin Radvan, president of Mars Wrigley Confectionary, a valued mentor over many years and someone who believed in and helped advance the work described herein in ways that made it possible. Thanks to Bryan Ayling, Ian Burton, and Cedric Bachellerie, and to former Oxford business school dean Professor Colin Mayer, our valued friend and partner in advancing and teaching the model to the next generation of business leaders, and to his team and to the current dean, Dr. Peter Tufano. And thanks to a treasured partner and confidant, the late Dr. Pamela Hartigan, director of the Skoll Centre for Social Entrepreneurship at Oxford, for her friendship, shared passion for the topic, and energetic drive to help us action the model in practical ways up until the very moment of her passing. She is greatly missed, but her memory lives on, in part via this work.

Last, but not least, we thank those who we have not specifically named herein who are nevertheless part of the journey to "complete capitalism," such as our writing coach in the early drafting stages, our other thought partners, the rest of our Catalyst team including several former Catalysts who contribute (or have contributed) in many ways, and our families and many friends and well-wishers who pray for us daily. Thank you all for what you are doing to unleash the transformational power of business to heal. We are humbled and privileged to be walking alongside you.

Index

Note: Page numbers in italics indicate figures; those ending in "t" indicate tables.

Index

181

About the Authors

Bruno Roche and Jay Jakub have been working side by side at Mars, Incorporated—makers of iconic brands like M&Ms, Snickers, Uncle Ben's, Pedigree, Wrigley's gum, and many more—for the last decade. They have worked together in the company's unique internal corporate "incubator" called Catalyst, established in the 1960s to challenge conventional business thinking by anticipating and identifying the next "big ideas" for business, then developing breakthrough capabilities to solve some of the corporation's most complex business challenges with advances that have transformational impact. Their deep friendship extends far beyond the workplace and into the realm of transforming business at large into a force for the common good, and in promoting vocational calling among those searching for greater meaning and purpose.

Bruno was born and raised in Paris, France, and has been married for the last twenty-five years to Marianne (Bayle), with whom he has four children. Both Bruno and Marianne trace their family lineages to the southern French village of Le Chambon sur Lignon, made famous by the heroism of the Huguenot villagers who saved the lives of countless Jews by hiding them during the Nazi occupation of France—an act for which the town is memorialized in the Yad Vashem Holocaust Center in Israel and upon which the documentary Weapons of the Spirit is based. Bruno has spent nearly three decades at Mars, mostly based in Brussels, Belgium, but traveling extensively to enact his unit's global remit. In addition to his Catalyst managing director function, he serves as Mars' chief economist. His education and academic research followed an applied mathematics path with a specialization in international finance, economics, and management sciences. He is fluent in French, English, and Italian. Bruno is a member of the World Economic Forum's Network of Global Agenda Councils (on Sustainable Development), and he served as a special advisor to the G20 during the term of the organization's French presidency (2009–2011).

Jay was born in Rahway, New Jersey—ironically also the hometown of economist Milton Friedman, founding father of financial capitalism—and has been married for the last thirty-one years to Eleni (Xanthakos), with whom he has two teenage children. Prior to joining Bruno at Mars in 2007, Jay had a long, distinguished government career in the US executive and legislative branches spanning nearly seventeen years, during which he held a number of senior positions. At Catalyst, Jay is the senior director of external research and co-manages with Bruno the unit's Mutuality Laboratory. He oversees the work of its Culture Laboratory and directs the external research partnerships Catalyst has forged with Oxford University's Saïd Business School and with leading academics around the world. His doctorate is from St. John's College, Oxford University, and he is the author of Spies and Saboteurs (MacMillan and St. Martin's Press, 1999).

Bruno and Jay, with their spouses, share a passion for people, especially the impoverished and oppressed, with a special focus on those who are broken in body, mind, and spirit. Completing Capitalism is their first joint book.

Berrett–Koehler
Publishers

Berrett-Koehler is an independent publisher dedicated to an ambitious mission: *Connecting people and ideas to create a world that works for all.*

We believe that the solutions to the world's problems will come from all of us, working at all levels: in our organizations, in our society, and in our own lives. Our BK Business books help people make their organizations more humane, democratic, diverse, and effective (we don't think there's any contradiction there). Our BK Currents books offer pathways to creating a more just, equitable, and sustainable society. Our BK Life books help people create positive change in their lives and align their personal practices with their aspirations for a better world.

All of our books are designed to bring people seeking positive change together around the ideas that empower them to see and shape the world in a new way.

And we strive to practice what we preach. At the core of our approach is Stewardship, a deep sense of responsibility to administer the company for the benefit of all of our stakeholder groups including authors, customers, employees, investors, service providers, and the communities and environment around us. Everything we do is built around this and our other key values of quality, partnership, inclusion, and sustainability.

This is why we are both a B-Corporation and a California Benefit Corporation—a certification and a for-profit legal status that require us to adhere to the highest standards for corporate, social, and environmental performance.

We are grateful to our readers, authors, and other friends of the company who consider themselves to be part of the BK Community. We hope that you, too, will join us in our mission.

A BK Business Book

We hope you enjoy this BK Business book. BK Business books pioneer new leadership and management practices and socially responsible approaches to business. They are designed to provide you with groundbreaking and practical tools to transform your work and organizations while upholding the triple bottom line of people, planet, and profits. High-five!

To find out more, visit **www.bkconnection.com.**

Berrett–Koehler
Publishers

Connecting people and ideas
to create a world that works for all

Dear Reader,

Thank you for picking up this book and joining our worldwide community of Berrett-Koehler readers. We share ideas that bring positive change into people's lives, organizations, and society.

To welcome you, we'd like to offer you a free e-book. You can pick from among twelve of our bestselling books by entering the promotional code **BKP92E** here: http://www.bkconnection.com/welcome.

When you claim your free e-book, we'll also send you a copy of our e-newsletter, the *BK Communiqué*. Although you're free to unsubscribe, there are many benefits to sticking around. In every issue of our newsletter you'll find

• A free e-book
• Tips from famous authors
• Discounts on spotlight titles
• Hilarious insider publishing news
• A chance to win a prize for answering a riddle

Best of all, our readers tell us, "Your newsletter is the only one I actually read." So claim your gift today, and please stay in touch!

Sincerely,

Charlotte Ashlock
Steward of the BK Website

Questions? Comments? Contact me at bkcommunity@bkpub.com.